THE STORY OF GOD
An Epic Journey through Scripture

Eric Geiger

THE STORY OF GOD
An Epic Journey through Scripture

© 2023 Rooted Network

Unless otherwise indicated, all Scripture quotations are from The Christian Standard Bible. Copyright © 2020 by Holman Bible Publishers. Used by permission. Christian Standard Bible®, and CSB® are federally registered trademarks of Holman Bible Publishers, all rights reserved.

Printed in China.

Table of Contents

About the Author	5
About the Study	6
Week 0: Getting Started	8
Week 1: Creation and Fall	10
The Story of God Timeline	14
Week 2: Promise and a People	24
Week 3: Rescue and Law	40
Week 4: Land and Kingdom	56
Experience: Break the Cycle	72
Week 5: Exile and Return	74
Week 6: Jesus	90
Week 7: A New People	108
Week 8: A Better Beginning	124
Experience: Join the Story	144
Deep(er) Dive	146
Appendix A: The 7 Rhythms of a Disciple	148
Appendix B: Experiential Discipleship	150
Appendix C: FAQs	153
Appendix D: Words Theologians Use When Talking about Scripture	154
Appendix E: Chronological Reading Plan	156
Additional Reading	162

About the Author

Eric Geiger

Eric Geiger is the Senior Pastor of Mariners Church in Irvine, California. Before moving to Southern California, Eric served as senior vice-president for Lifeway Christian Resources. Eric received his doctorate in leadership and church ministry from Southern Seminary. Eric has authored or co-authored several books including the best-selling church leadership book, *Simple Church*.

Eric is married to Kaye, and they have two daughters: Eden and Evie. During his free time, Eric enjoys dating his wife, taking his daughters to the beach, and playing basketball.

About the Study

Deep Dive
This series of Bible studies began as courses led by pastors in the local church. The people's enthusiastic response marked a pivotal moment of intentional disciple making and ongoing spiritual growth.

The intent for Deep Dive studies is to be immersed in a topic without being overwhelmed by it—providing theological depth with a pastoral heart. Like all Rooted Network resources, Deep Dive studies provide intentional opportunities for people to step out of their comfort zones and into spiritual growth.

The Story of God
The Story of God is an 8-week, group-discipleship resource exploring the overarching redemptive narrative of the Bible. Participants will discover that the story of Jesus is present on every page of Scripture and how they are to to live as part of that story. This chronological journey from Genesis to Revelation will remove the intimidation factor of reading the Bible and replace it with a passionate understanding of day-to-day life as followers of Jesus.

How to Use
You can begin with the teaching and discussion in Week 1; however, you may choose for *The Story of God* to be a 10-week experience by meeting for Week "0" and for sharing stories after Week 8. Week 0 is a time to set expectations, get to know one another, distribute workbooks, and provide instructions. The group discipleship experiences are times to put into practice what you've been learning. Meeting one last time to review the group discipleship experience and the previous weeks of study is a powerful way to make the most of your Deep Dive experience.

The Story of God will focus on both "word and deed" (Col. 3:17). The truths covered in this Deep Dive study are important doctrinally and practically. Our goal as disciples and disciple makers is to glorify Christ in every part of our lives, including *orthodoxy* (right doctrine) and *orthopraxy* (right practice).

Daily Devotions
This workbook includes four daily devotions and one day for personal reflection between group sessions. Time together will be more meaningful for everyone when each person comes ready to engage with the content and with each other.

Teaching
Each week has essential teaching videos for the group session. An outline of key points is provided in the workbook along with space to take notes. Follow the steps on the last page of this workbook to access *The Story of God Teaching Videos*. Stream the teaching videos each week from the Rooted Network Digital Hub.

Discussion
A discussion guide is provided on the pages following the teaching outline and notes. Since groups will have different needs, dynamics, and time constraints, use each guide as a tool, not a checklist. Feel free to use any of the questions that fit naturally into your conversation, skipping any that don't, and adding comments or questions of your own, in order to facilitate a meaningful interaction with the material and with other group members.

If time is limited, focus on:
- **an opening question to engage everyone,**
- **a question related to the biblical text,**
- **a review question about the teaching or personal study,**
- **and the application question for the takeaway.**

Allow plenty of time for each week's takeaway and how that truth applies to a daily life of faith in action. If you only have time to discuss one thing, the final question related to the takeaway touches on both understanding and application (orthodoxy and orthopraxy).

Finally, you'll notice that one biblical text is printed in the guide to anchor each discussion. Additional prompts will ask volunteers to look up and read other verses. While it's convenient to have scriptures printed for easy reference, it's also important to encourage the habit of people opening the Bible for study and discussion. God's Word has authority over our lives and we all want to hear from Him during this time together.

Experiences
We are committed to experiential learning at every stage in the disciple-making journey. This Deep Dive study includes discipleship experiences following Weeks 4 and 8.

WEEK 0

> "Then Jesus took them through the writings of Moses and all the prophets, explaining from all the Scriptures the things concerning himself. Luke 24:27 (NLT)

> "It is possible to know Bible stories, yet miss the Bible story.
> —Edmund Clowney

Getting Started

BEFORE gathering for the first group discussion, it's essential that everyone in the group...
- has a copy of this book AND...
- completes the personal study.

EACH WEEK, group members agree to...
- pray for one another,
- complete the four days of personal study,
- come prepared to engage in the teaching and discussion,
- seek a deeper understanding of life as a disciple and disciple maker,
- risk stepping out of their comfort zones in order to experience spiritual growth.

Make note of your group members' names and contact information. This will provide a helpful tool for communication, fellowship, and prayer.

NAMES   **CONTACT**

WEEK 1

PERSONAL BIBLE STUDY

A.W. Tozer famously said, "Nothing less than a whole Bible can make a whole Christian." While we will not go through every verse in the Bible in this study (it would be much longer than eight weeks), we will walk through the whole story of the Bible. So go ahead and preview the timeline and overview on the following pages before our first class so that you have a framework for where we're headed.

Simply put, the Bible is the story of God.

There is not a greater story. No other story has a hero like the Hero in this Story. No other story has a greater rescue than the rescue we find in this Story. No other story ends like this Story ends.

Sure, the world offers us other stories and other pursuits, but they all pale in comparison to this one. To Christ's Story. And whenever we chase those pursuits, we are chasing something less.

As you understand the whole Bible story, I believe the Lord will do a great work in your heart. I believe this because He did a great work in mine as I prepared and studied. I walked away from this time with a greater understanding of who He is and where I fit in the story He has been telling.

All the stories in my life, and all the stories in the Bible, make much more sense when I keep the Story of the Bible in view. So, I hope you throw yourself into this study, into the teaching times, into the devotions, and into the discussions with your group.

I am honored to be alongside you in this journey!

Eric Geiger

Before You Begin This Journey

How would you rate your comfort level with reading the Bible? (1 = lowest, 10 = highest)

1   **2**   **3**   **4**   **5**   **6**   **7**   **8**   **9**   **10**

Why did you rate yourself in this way?

Using the same scale, how would you rate your comfort level with talking about the Bible?

1   **2**   **3**   **4**   **5**   **6**   **7**   **8**   **9**   **10**

Why did you rate yourself in this way?

What do you hope to gain from this Deep Dive study?

The following timeline will help you personally prepare for the first session.

Prayerfully engage with the readings before coming to group each week for the Deep Dive teaching and group discussion.

The Story of God Timeline

| 2000 BC | 1400 BC | 1000 BC |

Creation and Fall | **Promise and a People** | **Rescue and Law** | **Land and Kingdom**

The self-sufficient and eternal God lovingly creates a perfect creation with humanity as His crowning work. Falling for Satan's temptation, humanity rebels and sin enters the world bringing death, pain, and strife. Instead of giving up on humanity, God promises that from the womb of a woman will come the One who will crush Satan's head.

God pursues Abram (who is renamed Abraham) a man from an idol-worshiping family who has no children with his wife, and promises that he will be the father of many nations. God promises land to Abraham and assures him that all nations will be blessed through his offspring. God continues to be faithful to this family. He restates the promise to Abraham's son Isaac and grandson Jacob (who is renamed Israel). A famine strikes the promised land, so Jacob and the family move to Egypt where one of his sons, Joseph, is already there to provide for them.

The family becomes a nation while living in Egypt, but also becomes enslaved to the Egyptians. God raises up Moses to lead His people to freedom. During a tenth plague, God strikes dead the firstborn son of everyone living in Egypt, but "passes over" Israel as they put the blood of lambs on their doorposts. After miraculously rescuing His people, God gives His people the law. He also instructs them to build a tabernacle and offer sacrifices so He may dwell among them.

God brings His people, through their leader Joshua, into the promised land. When God's people worship the gods of the nations surrounding them, God disciplines them through the attacks of surrounding nations. God raises up judges (or rulers) to rescue His people and call them to repentance. They beg for a king to be like other nations, and God gives them Saul. God then raises up a new king, David, and promises that his kingdom will never end. The family that turned into a nation is now a kingdom. David's son, Solomon, builds a temple to replace the tabernacle.

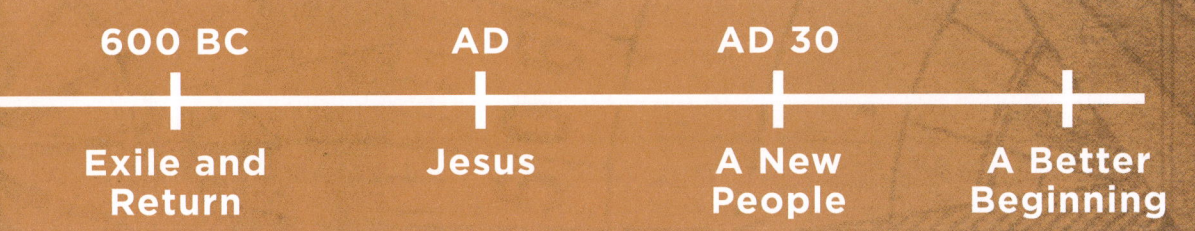

600 BC	AD	AD 30	
Exile and Return	Jesus	A New People	A Better Beginning

Solomon takes foreign wives and allows their foreign gods to clutter the land. His son continues the line of rulers and the kingdom is divided into the Northern Kingdom (Israel) and the Southern Kingdom (Judah). Prophets confront the people but they persist in their idolatry. The Northern Kingdom falls to Assyria and the Southern Kingdom is carried away into Babylonian captivity. When they are freed, they return to a nation and kingdom far less glorious than before and are still unable to keep their promises.

A descendant of Adam, Abraham, and David, Jesus is the One who crushes the head of Satan, will bless all nations, and reigns forever. Jesus, the God-Man, enters humanity through the womb of a virgin, perfectly obeys the law that we could never obey, dies as the once-and-for-all sacrifice for our sins, and rises from the dead, conquering Satan, sin, and death. He inaugurates His eternal kingdom and secures salvation for His people.

After His ascension to heaven, Jesus sends the promised Holy Spirit and His disciples turn the world upside down preaching the good news of Jesus. This good news is known as the gospel. In the midst of intense persecution, the gospel spreads, and Gentiles and Jews form a new people. Churches are planted in cities, and apostles write letters encouraging and instructing the people in the grace of Christ and their response to His grace.

A time is coming when God's people—people from every tribe, tongue, and nation who have been rescued by Christ—will enjoy Him and His rule forever in perfect harmony. Satan will be crushed, the effects of sin will be reversed, and all things will be made new.

Week 1: Creation and Fall

SCRIPTURES
Daily Devotional Reading

As a chronological overview of the Bible from start to finish, this Deep Dive study includes select passages from Genesis through Revelation. Each week, four days of personal study and one day of prayerful reflection will guide you from one group session to the next. These days of personal study and reflection are moments between the points on our timeline—connecting the dots to help you see the bigger picture of Scripture.

This first week will ease you into the story with just four scriptures setting the stage for our epic journey. Weeks 2-8 will dive deeper into each day's personal study. Ideally, you'll have time to read one passage of Scripture each day in the week leading up to the first group session. If you didn't receive your book in advance, that's OK—read what you can before your first discussion begins.

 Read Genesis 1:1–2:3.

Why is it important for your understanding of God and His story to start "in the beginning" with creation?

What verse, phrase, or truth stood out in Genesis 1:1–2:3?

 Read Psalm 96.

How does this psalm describe God in relation to the world?

What verse, phrase, or truth stood out in Psalm 96?

Read Psalm 139.

How does this psalm deepen your understanding of a personal relationship with the Creator?

What verse, phrase, or truth stood out in Psalm 139?

Read Isaiah 55:6–11.

What does God reveal about Himself in this prophetic text? Do you see it as a warning, invitation, or promise? Explain your answer.

What verse, phrase, or truth stood out in Isaiah 55:6–11?

REFLECT

 Before attending the group session, look back over the survey, timeline, and suggested scripture reading. Use this space to write down any thoughts, questions, or prayers related to your study of the Bible's one overarching story.

GROUP SESSION

WEEK 1

Creation and Fall

In this week's time together as a group, we'll consider how the beginning of a story is important for understanding the rest of it. The introduction of God, humanity, and the ongoing drama of history are found in the opening pages of the Bible. The story of God begins in Genesis and sets the stage for the rest of Scripture—including where we fit into His story today.

 Open your time together in prayer, asking God to help you understand and apply the truth revealed in His Word.

LEADERS: Sign in to the Rooted Network Digital Hub to stream this week's teaching video (internet connection is required). Your unique access code and a QR code linking to the Hub can be found on the last page of this workbook.

EVERYONE: Use the following pages for notes and group discussion.

Week 1 Teaching Outline

Scripture is the story of God because He wants you to know Him.

Introducing God . . . Five Truths:

    1. He is.

    2. He is the Creator.

    3. He is self-sufficient.

    4. He is gracious and loving.

    5. He is powerful and wise.

Introducing Us . . . Three Things We Learn:

    1. We were created to reflect His image.

    2. We were created to rule over creation.

    3. We were created to relate to others.

The Disaster We Made . . . Two Thoughts:

    1. Instead of reflecting His image, we rebelled.

    2. Instead of us ruling over creation, creation ruled over us.

Thank God the story doesn't end here. There is hope.

Protoevangelion: the first announcement of the gospel

NOTES

Discussion Guide

Groups will have varying amounts of time for discussion. Use any of the following questions that fit naturally into your conversation, adding comments or questions of your own. Allow plenty of time for processing the "takeaway" each week.

1. What are some of your favorite stories? Why are those meaningful to you? How would you describe an epic story?

2. How does viewing Scripture as one epic story shape the way you read the smaller stories throughout the Bible? Did the timeline on pages 14–15 help you see the overarching story? If so, what was helpful?

3. What happens if we only view the Bible as anything other than the story of God? (For example: individual stories, rules, history, poetry, prophecy, etc.)

Read Genesis 1:1 aloud.

In the beginning God created the heavens and the earth.
Genesis 1:1

4. *Genesis* means *beginning*. Why is it important for us to understand the beginning of the Bible?

5. Which of the five truths about God is most difficult to understand? Which is the most encouraging? How does the way God is introduced in Genesis shape the way we should relate to Him?

Read Genesis 1:26–28 aloud.

Then God said, "Let us make man in our image, according to our likeness. They will rule the fish of the sea, the birds of the sky, the livestock, the whole earth, and the creatures that crawl on the earth."

> ***So God created man in his own image;***
> ***he created him in the image of God;***
> ***he created them male and female.***

God blessed them, and God said to them, "Be fruitful, multiply, fill the earth, and subdue it. Rule the fish of the sea, the birds of the sky, and every creature that crawls on the earth."
Genesis 1:26–28

6. Why is it so important for us to understand we are made in God's image?

7. How does Satan tempt us in a similar way that he did Adam and Eve?

8. How do we still allow creation to rule over us?

9. Explain the glimmer of hope found at the end of Genesis 3. How did God show grace to Adam and Eve? In what ways has God shown grace to you?

10. How did the suggested scriptures for Week 1 orient you for our study of the story of God? (See p. 16-18.) Which scripture was especially meaningful? Why?

   📖 The creation narrative in Genesis 1:1-2:3

   📖 Every nation praising the Creator in Psalm 96

   📖 The personal nature of a relationship with God in Psalm 139

   📖 God's declaration of His ways and words in Isaiah 55:6-11

   📖 Questions, hopes, or prayers noted in your personal reflection

11. How does today's takeaway affect your view of God, Scripture, and yourself—even when you make a mess of life?

Takeaway:
From the beginning of Scripture, we see glimmers of hope pointing us to Jesus.

Week 1: Creation and Fall

WEEK 2

24 The Story of God

PERSONAL BIBLE STUDY

This week, the story of God takes us from the creation of the world and humanity to the establishment of a new covenant people. As the story unfolds, we'll see how God is faithful to keep His promises from the very beginning. Genesis follows the family line of Adam, through Noah, and leads us to Abraham.

 WHERE WE'VE BEEN: CREATION AND FALL

The self-sufficient and eternal God lovingly creates a perfect creation with humanity as His crowning work. Falling for Satan's temptation, humanity rebels and sin enters the world bringing death, pain, and strife. Instead of giving up on humanity, God promises that from the womb of a woman will come the One who will crush Satan's head.

 WHERE WE'RE HEADED: PROMISE AND A PEOPLE

God pursues Abram (who is renamed Abraham) a man from an idol-worshiping family who has no children with his wife, and promises that he will be the father of many nations. God promises land to Abraham and assures him that all nations will be blessed through his offspring. God continues to be faithful to this family. He restates the promise to Abraham's son Isaac and grandson Jacob (who is renamed Israel). A famine strikes the promised land, so Jacob and the family move to Egypt where one of Jacob's sons, Joseph, is already there to provide for the family.

DAY ONE
Brokenness & Blessed Exchange

In the beginning of God's story, we saw Him lovingly create humanity. We were the crowning work of His creation, and everything was perfect. The second chapter in Genesis ends with a statement of peace:

This is why a man leaves his father and mother and bonds with his wife, and they become one flesh. Both the man and his wife were naked, yet felt no shame. **Genesis 2:24-25**

No shame. Can you imagine life with no shame?

No guilt from your past mistakes. No regrets over choices you made or did not make but wish you had. No grief over words you said or did not say. Absolutely no shame.

Of course, all that changed in the very next chapter of Genesis when humanity rejected God's rule. Sin entered the world and shame came along with it. Peace was broken. The entrance of sin into the world was not a minor adjustment to God's creation. It affected everything.

Read Genesis 3:8-19 to see the aftermath.

PEACE WITH GOD WAS BROKEN.
They hid from the LORD God among the trees of the garden. **Genesis 3:8**
Adam and Eve realized they were naked and hid from the Lord among the trees. Instead of running to God, they ran from him. The "no shame" in Genesis 2 was traded for shame, guilt, and remorse.

PEACE WITH EACH OTHER WAS BROKEN.
Your desire will be for your husband, yet he will rule over you. **Genesis 3:16**
Instead of caring for his wife, Adam turned on her. Like a little kid who points the finger at his sibling, Adam defended himself before God by blaming Eve. Clearly this is not the type of leader a man should be—shirking responsibility, shifting blame, and passively watching the Enemy tempt his wife.

As a consequence of her sin, God told Eve that there would be relational tension between her and her husband. If you're married, you have experienced this. But husbands and wives aren't the only ones to feel the strain. Office politics, broken friendships, and business relationships gone south are all examples of broken peace.

PEACE WITHIN OURSELVES WAS BROKEN.
***You will eat from it by means of painful labor all the days of your life.* Genesis 3:17**

God told Adam that work would now be filled with painful labor. As a Christian, you know that your job—even if it is an awesome one—will not ultimately satisfy you. Work does not quench because our souls can only be quenched by God.

PEACE WITH OUR WORLD WAS BROKEN.
***The ground is cursed because of you.* Genesis 3:17**

Because of the fall, all of creation bears the weight of corruption. Sin has ravaged our world, and you daily face the ramifications. Cancer, disease, natural disasters, unfruitful harvests, and death are all the results of living in a broken world.

Is there any solution for our brokenness? For the shame we now face?

How have you personally experienced the brokenness from the fall? Explain.

Thankfully we can read about the shame of Genesis 3 with our eyes fixed on Jesus. When the apostle Paul wrote about marriage several thousand years later—he referenced Genesis 2 to show us how Christ loves us. He wrote:

***For this reason a man will leave his father and mother and be joined to his wife, and the two will become one flesh. This mystery is profound, but I am talking about Christ and the church.* Ephesians 5:31-32**

The word mystery here does not refer to something too deep or complex to understand, but to something that was hidden in the Old Testament that has now been revealed for our understanding and enjoyment. And Paul made the mystery clear: "I am talking about Christ and the church." When one becomes a Christian, one is united with Christ. When Adam and Eve were first united, they felt no shame. When we are united with Christ in faith, there is no shame. Martin Luther called this the blessed exchange:

"Faith unites the soul with Christ as a spouse with her husband. Everything which Christ has becomes the property of the believing soul; everything which the soul has becomes the property of the Christ. Christ possesses all blessings and eternal life: they are thenceforward the property of the soul. The soul has all the iniquities and sins: they become thenceforward the property of Christ. It is then a blessed exchange commences."[3]

How has Christ turned hopelessness into hope in your life? How have you personally experienced that hope?

DAY TWO
More Strife, Better Blood

One of the devastating results of sin entering the world is relational strife, evidenced by hatred and even violence toward one another. We have all lived it. We have fought with our parents, our spouses, our children, and our friends. Anger has festered in our hearts and bitterness has robbed us of our joy. Growing up, we fought on playgrounds, gossiped in hallways, called people names, and even bit each other. We can be ruthless. All this began in the garden of Eden.

If only the sin would have stopped in the garden. But it didn't. It escalated. That's how it always works, apart from God's grace. We see this clearly just one generation after Adam and Eve's devastating choice. Their children evidenced the devastating and natural progression of sin.

Read Genesis 4:1-16.

Cain was furious because the Lord looked with favor on Abel's offering and not on his. So, despite the Lord's warning about being mastered by sin (v. 7), Cain killed his own brother.

Why did God not receive Cain's offering? What is really going on here? Some verses in the New Testament cast more light on the two brothers.

By faith Abel offered to God a better sacrifice than Cain did. By faith he was approved as a righteous man, because God approved his gifts, and even though he is dead, he still speaks through his faith.
Hebrews 11:4

For this is the message you have heard from the beginning: We should love one another, unlike Cain, who was of the evil one and murdered his brother. And why did he murder him? Because his works were evil, and his brother's were righteous.
1 John 3:11-12

God receiving Abel's offering and rejecting Cain's was not based on what they offered with their hands, but on the condition of their hearts. Abel offered in faith. Cain's heart was evil, and he proved his evil by killing his brother.

Is there a problem with our world? Are things really that broken here? Genesis 4 shows us that, indeed, things are not as they were designed to be. The first son born into this world was a murderer.

Then [God] said, "What have you done? Your brother's blood cries out to me from the ground! So now you are cursed, alienated from the ground that opened its mouth to receive your brother's blood you have shed."
Genesis 4:10-11

What current events show that things are not as God designed them to be? Explain.

Cain's sinful rage caused him to spill the blood of his brother, and that blood condemned him. By God's grace, we have a rescue from this sin, from this hatred! The New Testament tells us that the blood of Jesus speaks a better word, a different word than the blood of Abel.

... to Jesus, the mediator of a new covenant, and to the sprinkled blood, which says better things than the blood of Abel.
Hebrews 12:24

Both Jesus and Abel were innocent and killed by sinful and hateful men. But their spilled blood speaks different messages. The blood of Abel condemned Cain; the blood of Jesus justifies us. The blood of Abel spoke against Cain; the blood of Christ speaks for us. The blood of Abel cries out for Cain's condemnation; the blood of Christ cries out for our forgiveness and justification.

We have been like Cain. We have hated, been angry, acted cruelly, and held bitterness and jealously in our hearts. Thankfully, Jesus' blood speaks a better word! We are not condemned. As Jesus' blood fell to the ground, our liberation and salvation were secured. We are not sent to wander the land but are welcomed to Him.

Consider a recent time that your life reflected Cain's response. If you've not repented for this thought or action, take time now to do so. Then, thank God that the blood of Christ has rescued us from condemnation for our sins.

DAY THREE
Cosmic Reboot

The space allocated in the Bible to the account of Noah (four chapters) indicates it is a significant event in the story God is telling. When you read the first six chapters of Genesis, you may think, *Wow, that escalated quickly*. In Genesis 2, everything is perfect. God had created everything, declared it to be good, and told Adam and Eve to multiply and steward creation. They enjoyed God and each other in perfect harmony. There was no shame, no sin, no pain, and no death.

Then Adam and Eve rebelled, and their cosmic rebellion had an impact on everything. We still feel the effects. Adam represents all of us, for all of us have sinned. The image of God is still in us, but it is distorted. Following the sin of Cain, who murdered his brother, sin spread rampantly. And already by Genesis 6, God has had enough.

When the LORD saw that human wickedness was widespread on the earth and that every inclination of the human mind was nothing but evil all the time, the LORD regretted that He had made man on the earth, and he was grieved in his heart . . . Noah, however, found favor with the Lord.
Genesis 6:5-8

Noah was not a perfect man, but God expressed grace to him and his family. Noah did not earn God's favor, but rather God graciously gave it to him. God told Noah to build a massive boat out of wood, an ark, so he and his family could be saved from the flood-waters that would destroy the whole earth. Noah and his family took pairs of animals and birds on the ark with them so that life would continue once the flood was over (Genesis 7:1-10). The flood was absolutely devastating.

The mountains were covered as the water surged above them more than twenty feet. Every creature perished—those that crawl on the earth, birds, livestock, wildlife, and those that swarm on the earth, as well as all mankind. Everything with the breath of the spirit of life in its nostrils—everything on dry land died. He wiped out every living thing that was on the face of the earth, from mankind to livestock, to creatures that crawl, to the birds of the sky, and they were wiped off the earth. Only Noah was left, and those that were with him in the ark.
Genesis 7:20-23

Sin violates God's holy character and must be punished, yet God is also loving and gracious. So to both punish sin and pardon people, God poured out His wrath through a flood while simultaneously using Noah and an ark to rescue people.

How do we see Christ in this story?

Centuries later Jesus came to be our pardon. Just as Noah saved his entire family from the just wrath of God, Jesus saved His family—those who believe in Him—from the punishment for sin.

After Noah and his family were saved and left the ark, Noah built an altar and offered sacrifices to God. Then God made a covenant with Noah and promised to never flood the whole earth again. This is the first time we see covenant used in God's story. A covenant is an agreement backed with a promise.

Then Noah built an altar to the LORD. He took some of every kind of clean animal and every kind of clean bird and offered burnt offerings on the altar. When the LORD smelled the pleasing aroma, He said to Himself, "I will never again curse the ground because of man, even though man's inclination is evil from his youth."
Genesis 8:20-21

Then God said to Noah and his sons with him, "Understand that I am establishing my covenant with you and your descendants after you, and with every living creature that is with you—birds, livestock, and all wildlife of the earth that are with you—all the animals of the earth that came out of the ark. I establish my covenant with you that never again will every creature be wiped out by floodwaters; there will never again be a flood to destroy the earth." And God said, "This is the sign of the covenant I am making between me and you and every living creature with you, a covenant for all future generations: I have placed my bow in the clouds, and it will be a sign of the covenant between me and the earth."
Genesis 9:8-13

Though hurricanes, tsunamis, and other disastrous effects of a fallen and broken world will still strike our world, the whole earth will never be flooded again. Every time we see a rainbow, we can remember that we have a God who keeps His promises.

As you close today, reread Genesis 9:7 and notice the command God gave Noah. God restated the command "Be fruitful and multiply," which He first gave to Adam and Eve in the garden (Gen. 1:28). God flooded the earth because of our sin, but He did not give up on humanity. He gave them a new start and continued to pursue them. Just as He continues to pursue us. Just as He continues to pursue you.

What evidence in your life shows that God has not given up on you?

DAY FOUR
More of Living for Ourselves

Just as God commanded Adam and Eve to be fruitful and multiply over the whole earth, He told Noah to do the same. But instead of multiplying and spreading over the whole earth, humanity chose to cluster together. Chronologically, the story of the tower of Babel fits sometime in the middle of Genesis 10—which gives us an account of the people who filled the earth. Before the people spread out speaking their own languages (Gen. 10:5), the following event took place.

The whole earth had the same language and vocabulary. As people migrated from the east, they found a valley in the land of Shinar and settled there. They said to each other, "Come, let's make oven-fired bricks." (They used brick for stone and asphalt for mortar.) And they said, "Come, let's build ourselves a city and a tower with its top in the sky. Let's make a name for ourselves; otherwise, we will be scattered throughout the earth."

Then the LORD came down to look over the city and the tower that the humans were building. The LORD said, "If they have begun to do this as one people all having the same language, then nothing they plan to do will be impossible for them. Come, let's go down there and confuse their language so that they will not understand one another's speech." So from there the LORD scattered them throughout the earth, and they stopped building the city. Therefore it is called Babylon, for there the LORD confused the language of the whole earth, and from there the LORD scattered them throughout the earth.
Genesis 11:1-9

The people in this story wanted community, security, and identity. They wanted community expressed in a city. They wanted security expressed in a tower that would protect them from others. And they wanted identity expressed in a name for themselves. They wanted good things for the wrong reasons and by the wrong means. Everyone wants to have a secure future, people who love them, and a sense of how and why they are on the planet. But these people wanted this for their own glory, and they were going to earn it themselves.

How have you sought community, security, and identity in the wrong ways? What were the consequences of your actions?

Building ourselves up runs in the same vein as Adam and Eve's sin. It speaks of wanting to be the ones who decide what is good and evil, reflecting our desire to be in charge.

So God divided the people into multiple languages and "scattered them over the face of the whole earth" (Gen. 11:8). Their desire to achieve community, security, and identity apart from God was halted since they could not complete their building project. The people were also pushed outward, spread across the land as God commanded
Genesis 1:28; 9:7

All this was in God's plan. Today, He doesn't receive worship in just one language, but many languages. And when His story concludes, He will be worshiped by people from every tribe, tongue, and nation (Rev. 5:9-10).

As we move forward to the next session, Genesis 12 will show us that God was going to bless all the nations through one man—a man willing to leave his community, his security, and his identity. He trusted God for all three instead of foolishly attempting to earn them on his own.

How have you found community, security, and identity in Christ?

REFLECT

 Before attending the group session, look back over the timeline and four days of personal study. Use this space to write down any thoughts, questions, or prayers related to your study of the Bible's one overarching story.

GROUP SESSION
WEEK 2

Promise and a People

In this week's group session, we'll see how God is faithful to keep His promises from the very beginning of Genesis by establishing a covenant with Abraham that continues to point to Jesus.

 Open your time together in prayer, asking God to help you understand and apply the truth revealed in His Word.

LEADERS: Sign in to the Rooted Network Digital Hub and stream this week's teaching video.

EVERYONE: Use the following pages for notes and group discussion.

Week 2 Teaching Outline

God often chooses the least likely people to accomplish His purposes.

To understand the story, we have to understand this family:

Abraham

     1. Abraham leaves.

     2. Abraham sleeps.

     3. Abraham laughs.

God always keeps His promises.

Isaac

Because of the sacrifice of Jesus, we are brought into this family of faith.

Jacob

We can't work our way to God; He comes to be with us. Jesus is the "ladder." (John 1:51)

NOTES

Week 2: Promise and a People

Discussion Guide

1. What reaction did you have to Eric's point about God often choosing unlikely people to accomplish His purposes? How might that be a key to understanding the whole story of God?

Read Hebrews 11:8-9 and 11:11-12 aloud.

8 By faith Abraham, when he was called, obeyed and set out for a place that he was going to receive as an inheritance. He went out, even though he did not know where he was going. 9 By faith he stayed as a foreigner in the land of promise, living in tents as did Isaac and Jacob, coheirs of the same promise.

**11 By faith even Sarah herself, when she was unable to have children, received power to conceive offspring, even though she was past the age, since she considered that the one who had promised was faithful. 12 Therefore, from one man—in fact, from one as good as dead—came offspring as numerous as the stars of the sky and as innumerable as the grains of sand along the seashore.
Hebrews 11:8-9, 11-12**

2. What did God call Abram to leave behind? What promise was made?

For clarity on the previous questions, look up Genesis 12:1-3 and read it aloud.

3. How would you explain the concept of covenant? How is a covenant different than a promise?

4. What is significant about the covenant ceremony in Genesis 15:17-18? Explain.

5. Why did Abraham and Sarah laugh at God?

6. How does the story of the sacrifice of Isaac point to Jesus?

For clarity on the previous questions, look up Hebrews 11:17-19 and read it aloud.

7. What has God asked you to leave or give up in order to follow Him in faith? What happened?

8. When have you laughed at God? What happened?

9. Eric shared a John Stott quote in today's teaching. How does it speak to what you've seen so far in Weeks 1 and 2 of our journey through Scripture?

Look back over the personal study.

10. What was especially meaningful or helpful in understanding the story of God and your life with Christ?

 Day 1: Brokenness & Blessed Exchange

 Day 2: More Strife, Better Blood

 Day 3: Cosmic Reboot

 Day 4: More of Living for Ourselves

 Day 5: Reflection

11. How does the takeaway affect your view of Scripture? How will you respond to this part of the story?

Takeaway:
God has done everything for us in Jesus, so we are part of His family through faith.

Week 2: Promise and a People

WEEK 3

PERSONAL BIBLE STUDY

The Christian faith is deeply connected to the family of Abraham. The God of Abraham, Isaac, and Jacob is also our God. From the lineage of Abraham comes Christ, and through Christ, people of all nations are made happy (blessed). Notice the timeline on the opposite page.

Abraham, approximately 2,000 years before Christ, points us to Christ. Then after Christ was crucified, resurrected, and ascended back into heaven, the New Testament writers referenced Abraham in their letters. During your personal study this week, press in so you can see how the faith and the family of this one man unfolds throughout the Bible, takes us to Christ, and matters for you today.

 WHERE WE'VE BEEN: PROMISE AND A PEOPLE

God pursues Abram (who is renamed Abraham) a man from an idol-worshiping family who has no children with his wife, and promises that he will be the father of many nations. God promises land to Abraham and assures him that all nations will be blessed through his offspring. God continues to be faithful to this family. He restates the promise to Abraham's son Isaac and grandson Jacob (who is renamed Israel). A famine strikes the promised land, so Jacob and the family move to Egypt where one of Jacob's sons, Joseph, is already there to provide for the family.

 WHERE WE'RE HEADED: RESCUE AND LAW

The family becomes a nation while living in Egypt, but also becomes enslaved to the Egyptians. God raises up Moses to lead His people to freedom. During a tenth plague, God strikes dead the firstborn son of everyone living in Egypt, but "passes over" Israel as they put the blood of lambs on their doorposts. After miraculously rescuing His people, God gives His people the law. He also instructs them to build a tabernacle and offer sacrifices so He may dwell among them.

Week 3: Rescue and Law

Salvation By Promise

When the apostle Paul wrote his Letter to the church at Galatia, he was writing to people who were confused on how one becomes a Christian and how one lives as a Christian. The Galatian believers had received Christ as Lord but were being falsely taught that they also needed to keep the law that God gave to Moses. (We will look closer at the law next week.) In the letter, Paul's message was clear, "You only need Christ!" and he used the promise God gave Abraham to prove his point.

Look at the timeline on page 12. Which did God give first: the promise to Abraham or the law to Moses? Why do you think that is important?

Read Galatians 3:15-18

Like many preachers, Paul grabbed attention with an illustration. Just as your grandparents' will cannot be changed after they die, the covenant God made cannot be changed. In other words, because the promise came before the law, the law does not change the promise. When God promised Abraham "all nations will be blessed by your offspring," God was announcing the gospel in advance. The offspring that brings the blessing to all nations is Christ.

As was mentioned in the second session, the establishment of the covenant between Abraham and God can be found in Genesis 15. In ancient days, when two people made a covenant, the practice was to take animals and cut them in pieces. Then the parties making the covenant would spread the pieces out on the ground and walk through them together to signify the seriousness of the arrangement. This symbolic action said, *If I break this covenant, may I be cut up like this animal was.* It was a graphic way to show how significant the agreement was. As both parties walked through the pieces together, they were saying, *I promise to fulfill my end of the deal, and if I don't, I am pronouncing judgment on myself.* But when it came time for the covenant ritual in Genesis 15, Abraham was asleep (Gen. 15:12,17-18). God walked alone through the sacrifice. He did all the work. Abraham was there, but he did nothing except believe. God alone fulfills the promise. The promise had nothing to do with Abraham's ability or his obedience. It was all about God's grace and faithfulness.

The same is true about salvation. It's all God's work. Sadly, many people don't really believe this. In a culture driven by achievement, many of us think we play a part in our salvation. We can even find it offensive when someone says we had nothing to do with our salvation, that we bring nothing to the table.

A research study by Lifeway Research found that 71 percent of Americans believe they must contribute something to their salvation. And 55 percent of people in evangelical churches believe this as well. This is tragic because salvation only comes from God. To think we played a part in saving ourselves is not to rely fully on His grace, on Christ. Like Abraham, we were asleep. We were dead in our sins, but God who is rich in mercy made us alive in Christ (Eph. 2:1-5). We could not fulfill our part of the covenant. God is the One who keeps the covenant for us.

William Temple said it well: "The only thing of my very own which I contribute to my redemption is the sin from which I need to be redeemed."

Have you ever found yourself trying to earn God's favor? Explain.

So you may be wondering, *If we are only made His because of the promise that Christ would come, what is the purpose of the law?* The apostle Paul anticipated the question and stated that the law came to point us to Christ. We cannot keep the law of God. We needed someone to keep it for us. We need the promise!

> **Why, then, was the law given? It was added for the sake of transgressions until the Seed to whom the promise was made would come.**
> **Galatians 3:19**

The law shows us we are sinful and need Christ to rescue us. If we receive Christ, putting our trust in Him, we are heirs of the promise. We belong to Christ and are part of Abraham's family. If you grew up in church, as a young kid you may have sung, "Father Abraham had many sons, many sons had father Abraham, and I am one of them ..." It's a pretty deep song for a six-year-old kid, but it's true. If your faith is in Christ, you are in Abraham's family. It is your faith that makes you right with God, not your race, your social status, or your gender. Only Christ.

> **There is no Jew or Greek, slave or free, male or female; since you are all one in Christ Jesus. And if you belong to Christ, then you are Abraham's seed, heirs according to the promise.**
> **Galatians 3:28-29**

When was the first moment you became aware of your sin and your need for God's grace? Did you respond in faith at that moment? Explain.

DAY TWO
Saved Just Like Abraham

Maybe you have wondered, *OK, I get that we are now saved by believing in Christ, but what about those people who lived before Christ came?*

Some have thought that perhaps those who lived before Christ were saved by their deeds, and now we are saved by our faith. But that cannot be true, for if someone could be saved by his deeds, then Christ died for nothing. We are saved by looking back to the cross and placing our faith in Christ. Those who lived before Christ were saved by looking forward and placing their faith in God's promise. We see this in Abraham's life. He did not earn God's favor; He simply believed the Lord, and his faith was credited as righteousness (Gen. 15:6).

When you hear the phrase "credited as righteousness," what do you think of? Why?

It's an incredible phrase. When writing to the church at Rome, the apostle Paul referenced Abraham's faith, using this phrase to explain what happens when someone becomes a Christian.

What then will we say that Abraham, our forefather according to the flesh, has found? If Abraham was justified by works, he has something to boast about—but not before God. For what does the Scripture say? Abraham believed God, and it was credited to him for righteousness. Now to the one who works, pay is not credited as a gift, but as something owed. But to the one who does not work, but believes on him who justifies the ungodly, his faith is credited for righteousness.
Romans 4:1-5

When Abraham placed his faith in God, God declared him to be righteous, meaning that Abraham was justified and made right with God. To be justified and to be made righteous essentially mean the same thing, deriving from the same root word in the biblical language. To help us get a better understanding, Jerry Bridges explained *justified* this way:

"There's an old play on the word justified: 'just-as-if-I'd never sinned.' But here's another way of saying it: 'just-as-if-I'd always obeyed.' Both are true. The first refers to the transfer of our moral debt to Christ so we're left with a 'clean' ledger, just as if we'd never sinned. The second tells us our ledger is now filled with the perfect righteousness of Christ, so it's just as if we'd always obeyed."

When you stop working to earn your salvation, when you stop attempting to stand before God in your own goodness and merit and trust Him instead—you are justified. You are made righteous.

Just as Abraham received righteousness by placing his faith in God, so do we. Not by our own efforts. Only through God.

God declares you to be righteous. What does that mean to you?

Do you know someone trying to be righteous by his or her own efforts?

What can you do to show that person the truth?

Week 3: Rescue and Law

DAY THREE
Isaac as an Illustration

Perhaps you have heard a guy at church give his "radically saved" testimony. The guy's story contains elements like drug addiction, random tattoos, laundering millions of dollars, and getting beat in and out of a gang. Maybe you felt that your testimony pales in comparison to his epic story. Yours is more like a testimony parents want their kids to have—a great Christian family, walking with the Lord from a young age, serving others rather than hurting them. More dull than radical. However, every person who knows Jesus has been radically saved. None of us were deader in sin than another, and none of us have been made any more alive than another. We were supernaturally born of God, not because of anything we did but because of His promise.

Have your ever experienced "testimony envy"? Explain.

The apostle Paul used the birth of Isaac as an illustration of what it means to be supernaturally born of God—to be a Christian. If you read this passage without knowing the whole Bible, without knowing the story of Abraham and Isaac, it is crazy confusing. It is hard to grasp even when you do know the story, but if you will press into the illustration, then you will better understand God's grace.

Tell me, you who want to be under the law, don't you hear the law? For it is written that Abraham had two sons, one by a slave and the other by a free woman. But the one by the slave was born as a result of the flesh, while the one by the free woman was born through promise. These things are being taken figuratively, for the women represent the two covenants. One is from Mount Sinai and bears children into slavery—this is Hagar. Now Hagar is Mount Sinai in Arabia and corresponds to the present Jerusalem, for she is in slavery with her children. But the Jerusalem above is free, and she is our mother. For it is written,
Rejoice, childless woman,
unable to give birth.
Burst into song and shout,
you who are not in labor,
for the children of the desolate woman will be many,
more numerous than those
of the woman who has a husband.
Now you too, brothers and sisters, like Isaac, are children of promise. But just as then the child born as a result of the flesh persecuted the one born as a result of the Spirit, so also now. But what does the Scripture say? Drive out the slave

and her son, for the son of the slave will never be a coheir with the son of the free woman. Therefore, brothers and sisters, we are not children of a slave but of the free woman.
Galatians 4:21-31

There is a lot going on in this passage, so maybe this chart will help:

THE LAW	GRACE
Abraham & Hagar	Abraham & Sarah
Ishmael	Isaac
Mt. Sinai "present Jerusalem"	Heaven (Jerusalem above)

Abraham and Sarah longed for a child. God promised them that they would have one, but as time passed, Sarah lost hope. In her impatience, she told her husband to sleep with one of her servants, Hagar. Abraham agreed to the plan and Hagar became pregnant. Hagar bore Abraham a son, and he named him Ishmael.

At this point, some might think God would write Abraham and Sarah off for not believing the promise and for taking matters into their own hands. But God did what He said He would do despite Abraham and Sarah's lack of faith. Though they were faithless, He remained faithful. Years passed, and Sarah finally did become pregnant. The couple named their son Isaac.

The two conceptions were very different from one another. Abraham and Hagar conceived not by trusting God, but by trusting themselves. They conceived in their own efforts. They couldn't wait for God's promise to be fulfilled. On the other hand, Abraham and Sarah conceived only because of God's promise. They were past the child-bearing years, so only in God's power were they able to have a child. It was supernatural in that it was the work of God, not the work of man.

The two children were very different from one another. Ishmael was the son of a slave. Isaac was the son of God's promise.

If you are a Christian, then you are a child of the promise and free. You are not a slave. You have been born of God. You are a miracle because you were dead in your sins, and God made you alive in Him. You were supernaturally brought to God because of His grace, not because you earned it.

Do you live as a child of the promise or as a slave? What's the evidence?

DAY FOUR
Abraham's Example

As you have seen thus far this week, the apostle Paul took readers back to both Abraham and Isaac in his letter to churches. He was not the only New Testament writer to do so. Matthew, James, Peter, and the writer of Hebrews mention Abraham as well. In both Hebrews and James, we see Abraham's faith held up as example. We have learned that Abraham was made right with God because of God, that he was not perfect and struggled just like we do. But we also see what faith looks like in this world, how we should live now that we have been made right with God. Today, study several of these passages and wrestle with the questions that follow.

By faith Abraham, when he was called, obeyed and set out for a place that he was going to receive as an inheritance. He went out, even though he did not know where he was going. By faith he stayed as a foreigner in the land of promise, living in tents as did Isaac and Jacob, coheirs of the same promise. For he was looking forward to the city that has foundations, whose architect and builder is God.
Hebrews 11:8-10

Abraham left everything to obey God. He traded familiarity for the unknown. He left comfort to follow the Comforter. What have you given up to follow God? What has your faith cost you?

Verse 10 gives us insight into what motivated Abraham to give up so much: "For he was looking forward to the city that has foundations, whose architect and builder is God." He was looking to the next life, not this one. The only way we can give up things in this world is if we believe in and long for the next one.

By faith Abraham, when he was tested, offered up Isaac. He received the promises and yet he was offering his one and only son, the one to whom it had been said, Your offspring will be traced through Isaac. He considered God to be able even to raise someone from the dead; therefore, he received him back, figuratively speaking.
Hebrews 11:17-19

If you are a parent, you know this story is staggering. God tested Abraham to see who was really on the throne of his life. Was it his son or was it God? Abraham lifted the knife to his boy because "he considered God able to raise someone from the dead" (Heb. 11:19). In other words, Abraham was not sure how this would work out, but he knew God was good, trusted Him, and believed if Isaac was killed that God could raise him from the dead.

God not only wants us to give up sinful things to follow Him, but He also wants to be above the good things in our lives. What good things must you constantly be sure don't become gods in your heart?

But someone will say, "You have faith, and I have works." Show me your faith without works, and I will show you faith by my works. You believe that God is one. Good! Even the demons believe—and they shudder.

Senseless person! Are you willing to learn that faith without works is useless? Wasn't Abraham our father justified by works in offering Isaac his son on the altar? You see that faith was active together with his works, and by works, faith was made complete, and the Scripture was fulfilled that says, Abraham believed God, and it was credited to him as righteousness, and he was called God's friend.
James 2:18-23

The apostle Paul pointed out that Abraham was justified by his faith. What you just read in the Book of James seems to say that Abraham was justified by his works, so this can seem confusing or contradictory. You have to look at the context. Mull over James 2:18 once again: "I will show you faith from my works." Works never lead to faith, but faith always leads to works. If we have true faith, our lives show it. Abraham believed God, received God's righteousness, and then showed his faith through his willingness to offer his son. Many have said, "We are saved by faith alone, but the faith that saves is never alone." True faith is always accompanied by works.

When you look at your life, where do you see works showing your faith? Explain.

REFLECT

Before attending the group session, look back over the timeline and four days of personal study. Use this space to write down any thoughts, questions, or prayers related to redemptive history and the Bible's one overarching story.

GROUP SESSION
WEEK 3

Rescue and Law

In this week's time together, we'll see how the covenant family line of Abraham, Isaac, and Jacob (Israel) becomes a nation while living in Egypt, but also becomes enslaved to the Egyptians. God raises up Moses to lead His people to freedom. After miraculously rescuing His people, God gives His people the law. He also instructs them to build a tabernacle and offer sacrifices so He may dwell among them.

 Open your time together in prayer, asking God to help you understand and apply the truth revealed in His Word.

LEADERS: Sign in to the Rooted Network Digital Hub and stream this week's teaching video.

EVERYONE: Use the following pages for notes and group discussion.

Week 3 Teaching Outline

Three ways God reveals His character:

1. God delivers HIs people.

2. God directs His people.

3. God dwells among His people.

How do we see Jesus in the book of Exodus?

1. Jesus is the I AM.

2. Jesus is the Lamb.

3. Jesus is the fulfillment of the law.

4. Jesus is the tabernacle.

5. Jesus is the greater Moses.

NOTES

Week 3: Rescue and Law

Discussion Guide

1. Share a quick summary of highlights from Weeks 1-2. Why is this week an important point in redemptive history and the unfolding story of God?

Read Exodus 3:13-15 aloud.

13 Then Moses asked God, "If I go to the Israelites and say to them, 'The God of your ancestors has sent me to you,' and they ask me, 'What is his name?' what should I tell them?"

**14 God replied to Moses, "I AM WHO I AM. This is what you are to say to the Israelites: 'I AM has sent me to you.'" 15 God also said to Moses, "Say this to the Israelites: The LORD, the God of your ancestors, the God of Abraham, the God of Isaac, and the God of Jacob, has sent me to you. This is my name forever; this is how I am to be remembered in every generation.
Exodus 3:13-15**

2. What is the significance of God's name as revealed to Moses (I AM)?

Read Exodus 2:24-25 aloud.

**24 God heard their groaning, and God remembered his covenant with Abraham, with Isaac, and with Jacob. 25 and God saw the Israelites, and God knew.
Exodus 2:24-25**

3. Why did God send plagues on the Egyptians?

4. What are some ways God delivered His people from Egypt? How does God still deliver?

Look up Exodus 20:1-17 and read it aloud.

5. How is "Do not have other gods before me" (Ex. 20:3) a gracious command? Explain.

6. How is the first command the key to everything else?

7. What are some things we worship besides God? Which of these causes the most struggle in your life? Why?

8. What was the purpose of the tabernacle?

9. Of the ways Jesus is shown in the Book of Exodus, which is most meaningful for you? Why?

Look back over the personal study.

10. What was especially meaningful or helpful in understanding the story of God and your life with Christ?

 Day 1: Salvation By Promise

 Day 2: Saved Just Like Abraham

 Day 3: Isaac as an Illustration

 Day 4: Abraham's Example

 Day 5: Reflection

11. How does the takeaway affect your view of Scripture? How will you respond to this part of the story?

Takeaway:
Jesus has rescued us from sin, so we trust that He loves us and we obey His commands.

Week 3: Rescue and Law   55

WEEK 4

PERSONAL BIBLE STUDY

During the first three days of this week's personal study we will zoom in on the timeline of events we covered in the Session 3 teaching: Moses receiving the law, man's inability to keep it, and thus man's need for a priest and sacrifices. Then the last day will take us forward in the storyline to God's people entering the land God had promised them.

 WHERE WE'VE BEEN: RESCUE AND LAW

The family becomes a nation while living in Egypt, but also becomes enslaved to the Egyptians. God raises up Moses to lead His people to freedom. During a tenth plague, God strikes dead the firstborn son of everyone living in Egypt, but "passes over" Israel as they put the blood of lambs on their doorposts. After miraculously rescuing His people, God gives His people the law. He also instructs them to build a tabernacle and offer sacrifices so He may dwell among them.

 WHERE WE'RE HEADED: LAND AND KINGDOM

God brings His people, through their leader Joshua, into the promised land. When God's people worship the gods of the nations surrounding them, God disciplines them through the attacks of surrounding nations. God raises up judges (or rulers to rescue His people and call them to repentance. They beg for a king to be like other nations, and God gives them Saul. God then raises up a new king, David, and promises that his kingdom will never end. The family that turned into a nation is now a kingdom. David's son, Solomon, builds a temple to replace the tabernacle.

DAY ONE
The Ten Commandments

When you think of the Ten Commandments, why do you think God gave them? What comes to your mind? Maybe you think of a teacher giving rules at the beginning of a school year. If you break one, you get your name on the board for every person to see. Or maybe you think of new employee orientation where you are given a policy book that is rarely read but somehow still legislates behavior. Because we tend not to like those moments, we can get a distorted view of the Ten Commandments.

God, however, is much better than the best teacher and much greater than the best place to work. He is our perfect and loving Father who gave the Ten Commandments to people He graciously and miraculously delivered from slavery. The commandments were given to God's people in response to who God is and the rescue He provided.

I am the LORD your God, who brought you out of the land of Egypt, out of the place of slavery.
Do not have other gods besides me.
Do not make an idol for yourself, whether in the shape of anything in the heavens above or on the earth below or in the waters under the earth. Do not bow in worship to them, and do not serve them; for I, the LORD your God, am a jealous God, bringing the consequences of the fathers' iniquity on the children to the third and fourth generations of those who hate me.
Exodus 20:2-5

I AM THE LORD YOUR GOD (WHO HE IS)
He is the One who is above all others, the Creator and Sustainer, the God above all gods and the King above all kings.

WHO BROUGHT YOU OUT OF THE LAND OF EGYPT (WHAT HE HAS DONE)
He is the One who rescued the people from their slavery, from the shame of being mistreated and abused, from the disgrace of being owned by the Egyptians. The Ten Commandments were given in response to their rescue from slavery, and they simultaneously pointed to the Rescuer (Jesus) who would come to deliver us from our sins. They point us to Jesus because the Commandments show us we need Jesus. We can't keep them! We need Him to keep them for us, to change our hearts, and to forgive us our sins.

The same is true for you. God's commands are given to you because of who God is and because He has rescued you from the slavery of sin.

Bible scholars and students often divide the Ten Commandments into two broad sections: commandments concerning our relationship with God and commandments concerning our relationships with others.

Read Exodus 20:1-17 and place the commandments in those two categories.

LOVE FOR GOD	LOVE FOR OTHERS

Let me guess, you want an answer key? Alright. The first four commandments deal with our relationship with God, and the following six commandments deal with our relationships with one another.

The first commandment is clearly about our hearts only bowing to the God who has rescued us. We shall have no other god—no other thing—besides Him in our hearts. He alone should rule and reign in our hearts because He alone rules and reigns over all things, and He alone has rescued us.

Martin Luther taught that if we break any of the commandments it is because we have already broken the first commandment, and if we keep the first commandment, we will keep all the others. For example, if we steal (violating the eighth commandment), it is only because we put the thing we are stealing ahead of God in our hearts. If we commit adultery, it is because we have put pursuit of a person ahead of God in our hearts. If we don't honor our parents, it is because we have stopped honoring our Father in our hearts.

The way we are motivated to keep the first commandment not to have any other god but Him is to continually be in awe that He is the Lord our God who brought us "out of the place of slavery," (Ex.20:2). As awe of Him and His rescue decreases, the burden to obey His commands increases. As awe for His rescue increases, the burden to obey Him decreases, and we want to obey Him because we love Him. This is love for God, to obey His commands, and His commands are not burdensome (1 John 5:3).

Is obeying God's commands burdensome to you? If so, why?

Take a few minutes to reflect on the great salvation that Christ has purchased for you. Consider the sacrifice He made and where you would be without Him. Let the awe and wonder of His great love fill your heart today.

Week 4: Land and Kingdom

DAY TWO
Broken Promises Already

Imagine that you are a young man or woman in the nation of Israel during the time when God's people were rescued from slavery in Egypt.

You grew up hearing your parents pray every night for rescue. You ran errands for Egyptian families with no payment and rarely any gratitude. You barely saw your father because he was always working on the Pharaoh's next building project.

Then one day a guy named Moses was speaking to a crowd outside your house. He said that God told him to tell the leader of Egypt to let Israel leave. You heard about this land promised to Abraham, Isaac, and Jacob. You longed to leave Egypt and slavery, but this seemed so random and utterly unlikely.

But when God started sending plagues as Moses promised, you believed. *Wow, we may actually be free soon!* you thought.

You helped your father put blood on the doors in preparation for the final plague. You struggled to get to sleep that night with anticipation of what was to come. Late in the night you woke up to wailing and crying throughout Egypt. Those without the blood of lambs on their doorposts lost their firstborn sons. It was so surreal, but you didn't have time to process because families were fleeing. There was great urgency and excitement: "We are free. Let's go!" The Egyptians were actually begging you to leave. They were terrified of displeasing your God anymore. You asked them for their possessions, as Moses instructed, and they actually gave them to you. You left Egypt with their gold and their silver. The gift of freedom was greater, but the gifts of gold and silver reminded you that God had orchestrated all of this. The God of Abraham, Isaac, and Jacob was your God, too, and He liberated you.

After rushing out of Egypt you came to the Red Sea. And as some feared, Pharaoh and the Egyptians were pursuing. You saw Moses lift up his hands and amazingly, the sea actually parted. It was terrifying and loud and awesome, but it was also clear that God was making a way for you to cross to safety. When you crossed and turned around, the waters fell on the Egyptians. Everyone cheered. Rescued again! You were in awe of the God who brought this about.

A few months later, Moses came down from a mountain where He had met with the Lord. You were eager to hear from the One who liberated you, who loved and protected you. Moses gave God's first commandment:

I am the LORD your God, who brought you out of the land of Egypt, out of the place of slavery.
Do not have other gods besides me.
Exodus 20:2-3

He then gave the second command:

Do not make an idol for yourself, whether in the shape of anything in the heavens above or on the earth below or in the waters under the earth. Do not bow in worship to them, and do not serve them; for I, the LORD your God, am a jealous God.
Exodus 20:4-5a

Of course! You nodded as you committed in your heart to give God and only God your worship. Only He deserves it. *Only He has rescued me*, you said to yourself.

Read Exodus 32:1-8 to see what happened.

After being rescued by God, the people found something other than God to worship. They took the gold the Lord gave them, the gifts from the Egyptians, and made a golden calf to honor, to give credit for their rescue from slavery.

In what ways do we often commit the same sin?

Whenever we look to something else other than God to give us our identity, our worth, or our ultimate satisfaction, we are committing the same sin of idolatry. Idolatry is placing something—anything—other than God on the thrones of our hearts. When we abandon the One who has rescued us and blessed us for something less than Him, we are bowing down to an idol, to something created and not the Creator. Everything that is not Him pales in comparison to the God who can say, "I am the LORD your God who brought you out of slavery. Do not have other gods besides Me."

What are the idols of our time? Which one do you struggle with the most? Why?

DAY THREE
Priests, Sacrifices, & the Act of Atonement

God gave His people the Ten Commandments in Exodus 20, including the commandments to not worship another god or make an idol. But shortly thereafter, the people were already bowing down to a golden calf. So God, in His mercy, set up a sacrificial system that would allow sinful man to approach our holy God.

God instituted an elaborate system where priests daily offered bloody sacrifices to God to serve as a temporary covering of sin. Every day priests were busy offering sacrifices for themselves and for others. In the Book of Leviticus, we find burnt offerings, sin offerings, grain offerings, fellowship offerings, and guilt offerings. The detailed instructions for sacrifices and offerings pointed people to the holiness of God and the reality that we cannot approach Him in our own merit.

All the sacrifices were designed to teach the people to loathe sin. With the constant sacrifices, people were confronted continually with the seriousness of sin. All the bloody sacrifices, all the noisy animals, would cause the people to hate their sin, to think, *My sin causes death. Every time I sin something dies.*

The sacrificial system would help people long for a Savior. The constant sacrifices reminded the people that they could not rescue or cleanse themselves. They needed a Savior whose blood was more sufficient than the blood of an animal.

All the daily sacrifices still were not enough, so God commanded a special Day of Atonement to be remembered annually.

Read Leviticus 16:1-10.

On the Day of Atonement, God instructed that two goats would be set apart. One of the goats would be slaughtered to signify that God's wrath was poured out on the sacrifice instead of on His people. The priest took the blood from the goat, brought it into the Most Holy Place inside the tabernacle, and sprinkled the blood on the lid of the ark of the covenant, also known as the mercy seat or the seat of propitiation. Inside the ark of the covenant, the Ten Commandments were stored. The people sinned against God's law, just as we have. So the blood being sprinkled on the seat of propitiation signified that God's wrath was being turned from His people and placed on the goat instead. Mercy was triumphing over judgment. The second goat was not killed. Instead of killing this goat, the priest would put his hands on the goat to symbolize that the sins of the people were transferred to the goat. The goat was then led to the wilderness and set free, symbolizing that the sins of the people were cast away from them. They were forgiven! Their sins could be forgiven because God's holy wrath was appeased.

One sacrifice symbolized that the wrath of God being satisfied. The other symbolized the sins of the people being removed from them.

Centuries later Jesus came, and He perfectly fulfilled the function of both sacrifices. When He placed Himself on the cross, willingly laying down His life for us, He placed Himself on the sacrificial altar. His body absorbed the wrath that should be ours, the wrath that we deserve. He also removed our sin from us.

The people could not keep God's commands, so an elaborate sacrificial system allowed them to approach God and enjoy His dwelling among them. We could not keep His commands either, so Jesus came as our sacrifice.

What was the purpose of the Old Testament sacrifices? Why were they not sufficient to forgive sin? How is Jesus the perfect sacrifice?

Victory Without a Fight

When God chose Moses to lead God's people to freedom, God not only promised their liberation from slavery, but He also promised He would give them the land He promised their forefathers Abraham, Isaac, and Jacob (Ex. 6:2-8). After wandering in the desert for 40 years after being rescued from their slavery, God's people were ready to move into the land of Canaan, the promised land. But the land was not vacant. Other people lived there, and those people needed to be conquered. God promised to drive out the other people not only because of His love for Israel, but also because of the wickedness of those living in Canaan (Deut. 9:4-5). The people living there were wicked; and they were not conquered until their sin "reached its full measure" before God (Gen. 15:16).

Moses' successor, Joshua, was the man God used to lead the people to conquer the land and divide it among God's people. But really God was the One who secured the victory. The first battle on the conquest made this absolutely clear. God handed over Jericho, a city in the promised land, to His people—to the nation of Israel.

Read Joshua 6:1-21.

Before the people in Jericho surrendered and without the Israelites raising a fist in fighting, God already called the battle: "I have handed Jericho to . . . you" (Josh. 6:2). Priests walked around the city, some carrying the ark of the covenant (where God made His presence known to man in the tabernacle), and seven carrying trumpets in front of the Ark. Troops were in front and behind the Ark, but they did nothing, not even shout. For six days they did this, and on the seventh day they marched, and Joshua told the people to shout when they heard the trumpets blast. They shouted and the walls crumbled. God gave Jericho to His people.

The story reminds us that God is attracted to weakness. In our individualistic culture, we often want to be strong. But in God's kingdom, weakness is strength. When we realize we are weak compared to Him, and that we, in our ability, cannot stand strong, God is attracted to our humility. He knows the proud from a distance, but the humble He knows up close (Ps. 138:6). Though we want to fight battles in our own strength, we must learn to walk quietly and allow the Lord to crumble the walls that He wants to crumble.

God is attracted to weakness. Do you agree with that statement? Why or why not?

What evidence do you see of this in the Scripture?

God continued to give every city in Canaan to His people. They moved into the land, divided it, and were finally home. Finally to the place the Lord had promised His people, first to Abraham, Isaac, and Jacob.

When they were in the land, the Lord reminded the people that He gave them the land and the victory. As Joshua reminded the people of their history, the Lord declared:

"I gave you a land you did not labor for, and cities you did not build, though you live in them; you are eating from vineyards and olive groves you did not plant. Therefore, fear the LORD and worship him in sincerity and truth. Get rid of the gods your ancestors worshiped ..."
Joshua 24:13-14

Because the Lord has rescued us, defeated sin for us, and fulfilled every single promise He has made, we are to fear Him and worship Him. And we are to get rid of the little gods that clutter our lives.

Do you have little gods cluttering your life? If so, take a moment to confess your sin, dethrone those gods, and let Christ take His rightful place as King of your life.

REFLECT

 Before attending the group session, look back over the timeline and four days of personal study. Use this space to write down any thoughts, questions, or prayers related to redemptive history and the Bible's one overarching story.

GROUP SESSION
WEEK 4

Land and Kingdom

In this week's time together, we see the cycle of God's ongoing faithfulness and His people's pattern of unfaithfulness. The young Hebrew nation worships the gods of the nations surrounding them, God disciplines them through the attacks of surrounding nations, raises up judges (or rulers) to rescue His people and call them to repentance, and He continues to be merciful and gracious. The family that turned into a nation is now a kingdom.

 Open your time together in prayer, asking God to help you understand and apply the truth revealed in His Word.

LEADERS: Sign in to the Rooted Network Digital Hub and stream this week's teaching video.

EVERYONE: Use the following pages for notes and group discussion.

Week 4 Teaching Outline

A clear pattern exists in the story:

1. God delivers on His promises.

2. God disciplines His people.

3. God decrees His purposes.

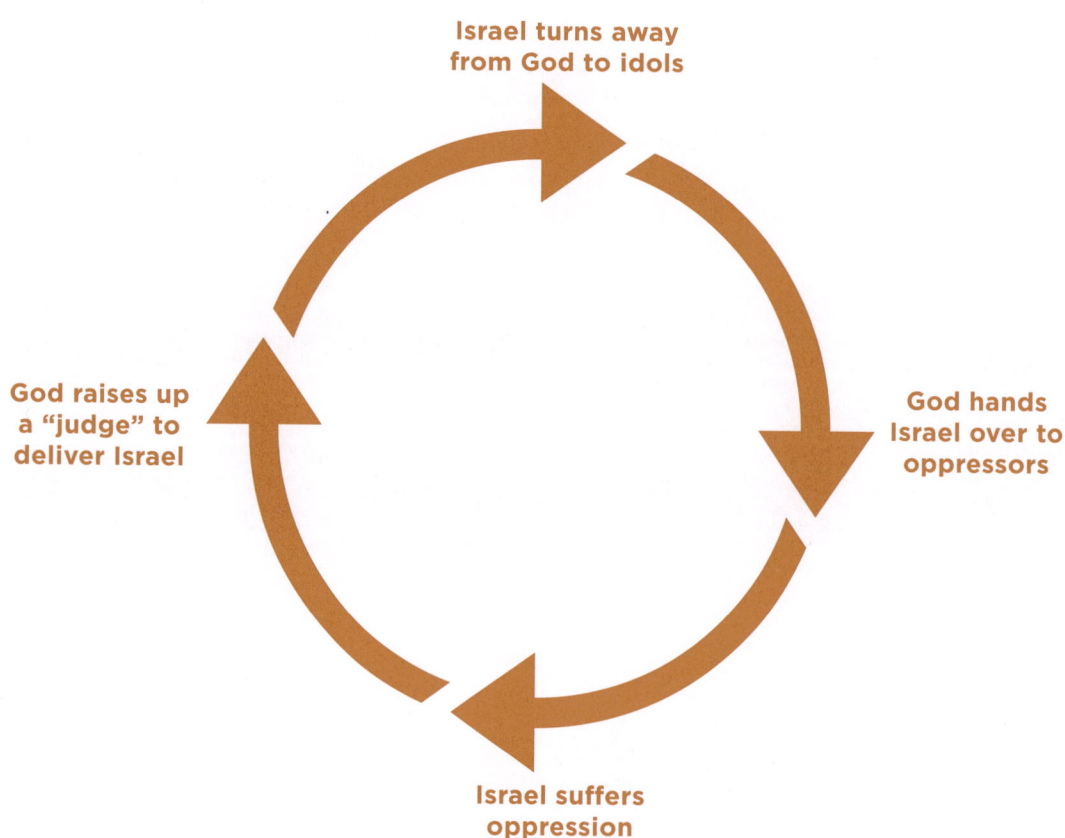

NOTES

Discussion Guide

1. Share a quick summary of highlights from Weeks 1–3. Why is this week an important point in redemptive history and the unfolding story of God?

Read Joshua 21:43–45 aloud.

43 So the LORD gave Israel all the land he had sworn to give their ancestors, and they took possession of it and settled there. 44 The LORD gave them rest on every side according to all he had sworn to their ancestors. None of their enemies were able to stand against them, for the LORD handed over all their enemies to them. 45 None of the good promises the LORD had made to the house of Israel failed. Everything was fulfilled.
Joshua 21:43–45

2. What does God delivering on His promises say about His character?

3. How have you seen God deliver on His promises? Explain.

Look up Judges 2:11–12 and 2:16–17. Read it aloud.

4. How do you struggle with the cycle of sin in your life?

5. Why does God hate sin? Why does God discipline His people?

6. How have you experienced the Lord's discipline in your life?

7. If you don't experience God's discipline, what does that indicate? Explain.

For clarity on the previous questions, look up Hebrews 12:6. Read it aloud.

Look up 1 Samuel 16:7. Read it aloud.

8. Are you a man after the people's hearts, like Saul, or a man after God's heart, like David? Explain.

Look back over the personal study.

9. What was especially meaningful or helpful in understanding the story of God and your life with Christ?

 Day 1: The Ten Commandments

 Day 2: Broken Promises Already

 Day 3: Priests, Sacrifices, & the Act of Atonement

 Day 4: Victory Without a Fight

 Day 5: Reflection

10. How does the takeaway affect your view of Scripture? How will you respond to this part of the story?

11. Be sure to complete the discipleship experience following this session. It's an important rhythm to develop for your life in the story of God.

Takeaway:
We have a place in God's everlasting kingdom because Jesus is a good King.

EXPERIENCE 1: BREAK THE CYCLE

 See Appendix B: Experiential Discipleship to prepare for this time of repentance.

Here is your opportunity to review what you have been learning and break the cycle of sin in your life. The word *repentance* can be a scary or confusing word for people, but it simply means turning away from the direction you've been going and turning around toward God instead—breaking the cycle of sin. Repentance is an act of choosing the freedom and renewed life made possible in Jesus.

This may mean turning away from your own patterns of sin and toward God for the first time. It may mean turning back to God as you stray from Him, whether it was knowingly choosing sin instead of God or growing more mature in your faith and recognizing things that distract you from following Jesus wholeheartedly. Either way, God welcomes you into a close relationship with Him.

No matter where you are on your journey of faith in Jesus, repentance is an essential rhythm we never outgrow because there will always be things pulling our hearts away from Him.

It is easy to learn about biblical stories and wonder why people kept rebelling against God or slowly forgetting His goodness. It's also easy to recognize this pattern in other people's lives. It's harder to be honest with yourself.

Look back over your answers and prayers so far in this book—what is God showing you? If you look at your own story lately, where are you in this cycle? You may be doing pretty well following Jesus in general, but there's a part of your life needing forgiveness and freedom.

One of the most powerful things you can do when breaking strongholds of sin and disbelief is to share your confession and repentance with trusted and mature people in your faith community. Allow them to pray for you and to celebrate God's work in your life.

If you need to ask for someone's forgiveness, be sure to clearly express how you were wrong and why you desire to make things right with them. Do not demand anything from them, knowing that it may take time to reconcile, for that person to recognize any way they may have also been wrong, or for them to even be willing to consider your apology.

Write down any strongholds God reveals, a prayer of confession and thanks for God's grace, and the names of people you need to share your repentance with.

Experience 1: Break the Cycle

WEEK 5

PERSONAL BIBLE STUDY

In the teaching for Session 4, we covered a lot of ground, from God's people moving into the promised land to the period of the judges. We also covered the reigns of Saul, David, and Solomon as kings of Israel. During this latter period in Israel's history, David wrote many of the psalms, and Solomon wrote Ecclesiastes, some of Proverbs, and Song of Solomon. This week's personal Bible study will give you a sampling of how this wisdom literature points to Jesus.

 WHERE WE'VE BEEN: LAND AND KINGDOM

God brings His people, through their leader Joshua, into the promised land. When God's people worship the gods of the nations surrounding them, God disciplines them through the attacks of surrounding nations. God raises up judges (or rulers) to rescue His people and call them to repentance. They beg for a king to be like other nations, and God gives them Saul. God then raises up a new king, David, and promises that his kingdom will never end. The family that turned into a nation is now a kingdom. David's son, Solomon, builds a temple to replace the tabernacle.

 WHERE WE'RE HEADED: EXILE AND RETURN

Solomon takes foreign wives and allows their foreign gods to clutter the land. His son continues the line of rulers and the kingdom is divided into the Northern Kingdom (Israel) and the Southern Kingdom (Judah). Prophets confront the people but they persist in their idolatry. The Northern Kingdom falls to Assyria and the Southern Kingdom is carried away into Babylonian captivity. When they are freed, they return to a nation and kingdom far less glorious than before and are still unable to keep their promises.

DAY ONE
An Imperfect King

The background to Psalm 51 is found in 2 Samuel 11–12. David had been a great leader, a man after God's own heart. He had administered justice and shown compassion. But things went terribly wrong in his life. Second Samuel 11 opens with David staying in Jerusalem alone while his men go off to war. David was restless at night. Instead of "gazing on the beauty of the Lord" (Ps. 27:4), David went to the roof and beheld the beauty of a woman—a married woman named Bathsheba. He called for her, slept with her, and she got pregnant.

Instead of coming clean about his sin, David planned an elaborate cover-up. He brought her husband, Uriah, home from war, believing he would sleep with his wife and all would be forgotten (there were not DNA tests in ancient Israel). Uriah came home from war but refused, even after David served him drinks, to go home to his wife because his fellow soldiers were sleeping on battlefields. So David sent instructions—in a sealed envelope that Uriah carried back to the battlefield with him—to Joab, his chief military leader. The instructions were to put Uriah on the field where the fighting was fiercest and remove the troops. Joab did so, and Uriah was killed. David had now committed adultery and murder.

Nathan, the prophet, confronted David in his sin with an epic illustration: Hey David, a rich man has an out-of-town guest and instead of killing one of his many animals for supper, he kills the one lamb of a poor man. David burned with anger and wanted to find this man and administer justice. Nathan responded simply, "You are the man!" (2 Sam. 12:7). David, because he belonged to the Lord, recognized his sin, repented, and sought God for forgiveness. Psalm 51 is his prayer of forgiveness.

Read Psalm 51.

Notice that David did not pray for his eyes in this psalm. He did not pray that God would protect him from looking at women, nor that the Lord would give him friends who would hold him accountable. He did not make bold promises to God that he would never sin again. He knew he was too broken to keep them. Instead, he prayed for God to clean his heart (v. 10). He knew his heart was the problem.

Psalm 51 shows us the depth of sin in our hearts. It reveals to us just how much in need of God's grace we are. In the first two verses, we see three different words that give us a comprehensive view of our sin.

*Be gracious to me, God,
according to your faithful love;
according to your abundant compassion,
blot out my rebellion.
Completely wash away my guilt
and cleanse me from my sin.
For I am conscious of my rebellion,
and my sin is always before me.*
Psalm 51:1-3

The three words describing the sinful depth of our own hearts are:

REBELLION (TRANSGRESSION)
In the original language, this word speaks of willful disobedience against the One to whom we owe our allegiance. Rebellion is our declaration to God that we will do things our way, not His. When David knew Bathsheba was married but pursued her anyway, this was rebellion.

GUILT (INIQUITY)
The word for iniquity carries the sense of shifting. Our hearts have shifted out of place. Instead of focusing on Him, we focus on lesser things. David, as he walked around one night, was looking for something other than the glory of God; therefore, he was susceptible to the beauty of a woman.

SIN
Sin means to miss the mark. When we sin, we miss the mark of God's holiness. When David lusted, he missed the mark of God's love. When he lied, he missed the mark of God's truthfulness. When he murdered, he missed the mark of God who is life.

The good news is that God is eager to forgive, blot out our rebellion, wash away our guilt, and cleanse us from our sin. Our sin is great, but God's grace is greater.

David's sin reminds us that, though he was a great king, he was still imperfect and broken. We all are, even the king who unified Israel and conquered their enemies. Thankfully another King came from the line of David—the perfect and conquering King Jesus who secured our forgiveness on the cross.

How can you relate to David's experience? Explain.

If you have unconfessed sin in your life, take time now to confess it to the Lord and ask Him to create in you a clean heart.

DAY TWO
The Joy of Forgiveness

The Psalms were compiled over hundreds of years and are not presented in chronological order. God's people read and sang them to remember God's faithfulness to His people. Even us public school kids can see that the 32nd Psalm comes before Psalm 51 in our Bibles, but scholars believe that Psalm 32 is David's celebration of his forgiveness after he prayed Psalm 51. So the order of these events is:

Read Psalm 32.

Yesterday we studied three words in Psalm 51 that show us the depth of our sin. In this psalm, we see three words that show us the greatness of our forgiveness. David was overwhelmed with the awesomeness of God's forgiveness. Of this psalm and the words showing our sin, Charles Spurgeon said:

"Note the three words often used to denote our disobedience: transgression, sin, and iniquity are the three-headed dog at the gates of hell, but our glorious Lord has silenced its barkings forever against his own believing ones. The trinity of sin is overcome by the Trinity of heaven."

The three words are found in the first two verses:

How joyful is the one
whose transgression is forgiven,
whose sin is covered!
How joyful is the person whom
the LORD does not charge with iniquity
and in whose spirit is no deceit!
Psalm 32:1-2

FORGIVEN

The word for forgiven in the original Hebrew (the Old Testament was originally written in Hebrew) means "carried away." How joyful is the one whose transgression is carried away! Your sin, if you are His, has been carried away.

If you, in your mind, are still carrying sin from your past—you are carrying a mirage. Your sin is no longer with you; instead, the Lord has carried it away.

COVERED

When we attempt to cover our own sins, we are like the foolish dog that uses the bathroom in your front yard and thinks two kicks with his back legs will cover up the mess. We cannot cover our mess, our sin. But if we uncover it, if we come to God with our sin, He covers it for us.

DOES NOT CHARGE

God's grace is amazing. If we are His, He does not charge us with sin. Instead He charges or credits us with His righteousness and forgiveness. In our place, Jesus was charged with our sin so we could be credited with His perfection.

Of this passage, Martin Luther said something very powerful:

"We are all sinners alike, only that the sins of the holy are not counted but covered; and the sins of the unholy are not covered but counted."

You are no better than anyone else. You have sinned as all people have sinned. But Christ has covered your sins and not charged you with them. Rejoice in that reality today.

How have experienced the forgiveness and restoration of God?

DAY THREE

Futility!

You have likely seen pictures of Stonehenge, massive rocks on the side of a beautiful hill. Generations of people have wondered how Stonehenge became Stonehenge. How did these massive stones end up where they are? One theory is that the stones were moved from a hill 150 miles away. To learn as much as possible about the stones and life surrounding them, archaeologists have been digging on that hill for 90 years. But in 2013, geologists discovered that the archaeologists have been digging on the wrong hill. The hill they should have been excavating is just over a mile away. For 90 years, they centered their lives on the wrong hill. Imagine the misery of learning you have squandered so much time in pursuit of the wrong thing.

In the Book of Ecclesiastes, Solomon—David's son and the king the Lord gave wisdom to—wrote that everything in this life, everything under the sun, is absolutely futile. While Solomon walked with the Lord, the Lord gave him great insight, and we have much to learn from him.

Read Ecclesiastes 1 and take note of all that is described as futile.

Which of these futile activities do you struggle with the most? Why?

We see the futility of laboring for accomplishments. Though the streams outlast us, they can never fill the sea. Generations come and go, and the earth remains, but no matter how hard the streams work, they cannot make the sea full. In other words, work done "under the sun" is really futile (v. 7).

We see the futility of laboring for pleasure. Though we have new things to look at and new sounds to hear, the eye and the ear remain unsatisfied. Pleasures never last. They are futile, too (v. 8).

We see the futility of laboring for legacy. OK, if working for accomplishments and working for pleasure are empty, what about working to leave behind a legacy? Futile. Generations from now, no one will remember you (v. 11).

We see the futility of laboring in blessing. Solomon tried to find joy in the blessing the Lord gave him, in his wisdom. But that too is folly and a pursuit of the wind (v. 17).

Laboring for accomplishment, pleasure, and legacy is futile. Even laboring and finding identity in the blessings of God is futility.

Why all this futility? I'm sure you're thinking, *Thanks for the motivation, Geiger.* Maybe you even thought, *This is borderline depressing*. It is important for us to understand the pain of a broken and fallen world, but also to know there is hope.

The word futile is used 38 times throughout the Book of Ecclesiastes, and only used one time in the New Testament. The apostle Paul explained why this life is filled with futility in Romans 8:20. He wrote:

For the creation was subjected to futility—not willingly, but because of him who subjected it—in the hope that the creation itself will also be set free from the bondage to decay into the glorious freedom of God's children.
Romans 8:20-21

Before sin entered the world, everything was perfect. It was not futile. But humanity sinned and all that humankind was responsible for (we were given responsibility over creation) suffered. Creation was subjected to futility because God judged creation as a result of our sin. But He also gave creation hope that there will be a day when all things will be made new. When Christ returns, He will rescue all of creation from futility.

Creation will one day be rescued from futility, and the same One who will rescue all of creation can rescue us from futility now. You don't have to be a man who lives under the sun, who lives for only this world. You don't have to dig on the wrong hill. Instead of laboring under the sun, we can rest in the One who came here for us—the One who did all the work for us on the cross, Jesus, who gives us rest from futility in this life. Only the King of kings can rescue us from the futility of futilities.

How would you define futile? In what ways do you get caught up in running after things that are futile?

Get Wisdom

When Solomon became king, he prayed for wisdom. God graciously responded:

Since this was in your heart, and you have not requested riches, wealth, or glory, or for the life of those who hate you, and you have not even requested long life, but you have requested for yourself wisdom and knowledge that you may judge my people over whom I have made you king, wisdom and knowledge are given to you. I will also give you riches, wealth, and glory, unlike what was given to the kings who were before you, or will be given to those after you.
2 Chronicles 1:11-12

Solomon is the major writer in the Book of Proverbs. The book was essentially the parenting manual for the people of God. Fathers would use the sayings with their sons to instill wisdom in young men. The book is extremely practical because wisdom impacts life today. Wisdom is the art of living life skillfully. You may have been blessed with the shepherding and counsel of a father or mother who parented you well, and these wise sayings sound a lot like the instruction you received. Or you may have heard counsel very different from these wise sayings. Either way, these sayings are for you now.

Reflect on these questions and proverbs today:

HOW IMPORTANT IS WISDOM?
Wisdom is supreme—so get wisdom. And whatever else you get, get understanding. Cherish her, and she will exalt you; if you embrace her, she will honor you.
Proverbs 4:7-8

WHERE DOES WISDOM COME FROM?
The fear of the LORD is the beginning of knowledge; fools despise wisdom and discipline.
Proverbs 1:7

WHAT IS MOST IMPORTANT TO LOOK FOR AS A SPOUSE?
Charm is deceptive and beauty is fleeting, but a woman who fears the LORD will be praised.
Proverbs 31:30

SHOULD I DO WHAT THE CULTURE/WORLD ADVISES?
There is a way that seems right to a person, but its end is the way to death.
Proverbs 14:12

DO I NEED BIBLICAL COMMUNITY?
Iron sharpens iron, and one person sharpens another.
Proverbs 27:17

WHAT HAPPENS TO THE PROUD?
Pride comes before destruction, and an arrogant spirit before a fall.
Proverbs 16:18

HOW SHOULD I SPEAK TO PEOPLE?
A gentle answer turns away anger, but a harsh word stirs up wrath.
Proverbs 15:1

SHOULD I WORK HARD?
Go to the ant, you slacker! Observe its ways and become wise. Without leader, administrator, or ruler, it prepares its provisions in summer; it gathers its food during harvest. How long will you stay in bed, you slacker?
When will you get up from your sleep? A little sleep, a little slumber, a little folding of the arms to rest, and your poverty will come like a robber, your need, like a bandit.
Proverbs 6:6-11

HOW SHOULD I VIEW DEBT?
The rich rule over the poor, and the borrower is a slave to the lender.
Proverbs 22:7

DOES MY REPUTATION MATTER?
A good name is to be chosen over great wealth; favor is better than silver and gold.
Proverbs 22:1

DO MY CLOSE FRIENDS MATTER?
The one who walks with the wise will become wise, but a companion of fools will suffer harm.
Proverbs 13:20

DO THOSE WHO CANNOT DEFEND THEMSELVES MATTER?
Speak up for those who have no voice for the justice of all who are dispossessed. Speak up, judge righteously, and defend the cause of the oppressed and needy.
Proverbs 31:8-9

What's the difference between wisdom and knowledge? Explain.

Who is the wisest person you know? Based on what?

Where do you look for wisdom? Is God and His Word your first choice? Why or why not?

REFLECT

Before attending the group session, look back over the timeline and four days of personal study. Use this space to write down any thoughts, questions, or prayers related to redemptive history and the Bible's one overarching story.

_____
_____
_____
_____
_____
_____
_____
_____
_____
_____
_____
_____
_____
_____
_____
_____
_____
_____
_____
_____
_____
_____
_____
_____

GROUP SESSION
WEEK 5

Exile and Return

In this week's time together, our final "season" in the Old Testament, we'll see the tragic state of God's people and another heroic salvation. The kingdom from last week has now been divided and conquered—the people taken into captivity. Once again, the people turn their hearts back to the ever-faithful God after experiencing the consequences of their own unfaithfulness. When they are freed, they return to a nation and kingdom far less glorious than before and are still unable to keep their promises.

 Open your time together in prayer, asking God to help you understand and apply the truth revealed in His Word.

LEADERS: Sign in to the Rooted Network Digital Hub and stream this week's teaching video.

EVERYONE: Use the following pages for notes and group discussion.

Week 5 Teaching Outline

The story continues with God's pattern of faithfulness:

1. God rebukes.

2. God remembers.

3. God restores.

There's a hopeless ending to the Old Testament, leaving us with a longing for the One to come—the ultimate cliffhanger. Hope is going to arrive and His name is Jesus.

Discussion Guide

1. Share a quick summary of highlights from Weeks 1–4. Why is this week an important point in redemptive history and the unfolding story of God?

2. How did Solomon compromise his devotion to God? Explain.

3. What in your life causes you to compromise your devotion to God? Why?

Read 2 Kings 17:7 aloud.

7 This disaster happened because the people of Israel sinned against the LORD their God who had brought them out of the land of Egypt from the power of Pharaoh king of Egypt and because they worshiped other gods.
2 Kings 17:7

4. What were the consequences for both Israel and Judah because of their idolatry?

5. What consequences have you experienced because of your idolatry? Explain.

Read Ezekiel 36:24-27 aloud.

24 For I will take you from the nations and gather you from all the countries, and will bring you into your own land. 25 I will also sprinkle clean water on you, and you will be clean. I will cleanse you from all your impurities and all your idols. 26 I will give you a new heart and put a new spirit within you; I will remove your heart of stone and give you a heart of flesh. 27 I will place my Spirit within you and cause you to follow my statutes and carefully observe my ordinances.
Ezekiel 36:24-27

6. How has God shown faithful love to you, even when you rebelled against Him?

7. What does it mean that God would replace the people's heart of stone with a heart of flesh? How has God changed your heart?

8. When have you experienced God's restoration? Be specific.

9. Why does the Old Testament end on a seemingly hopeless note? How does the story of God up to this point make you feel?

10. Have you ever experienced a season of silence, where you weren't hearing from God? How does that relate to the story of God so far?

Look back over the personal study.

11. What was especially meaningful or helpful in understanding the story of God and your life with Christ?

 Day 1: An Imperfect King

 Day 2: The Joy of Forgiveness

 Day 3: Futility!

 Day 4: Get Wisdom

 Day 5: Reflection

12. Look back at the *Break the Cycle* discipleship experience (p. 72–73). Has God revealed any more to you about patterns or strongholds in your life—especially in relation to this week's devotionals on sin, forgiveness, futility, and wisdom?

13. How does the takeaway affect your view of Scripture? How will you respond to this part of the story?

 Takeaway:
We are unable to keep our promises and need a new heart.

WEEK 6

PERSONAL BIBLE STUDY

The passages you will study this week chronicle events that happened during the period of history we covered in the Session 5 teaching. God's people were united under King David and enjoyed a season of peace and prosperity. But David's son, Solomon, compromised his devotion to God and pursued the gods of his wives and concubines. The nation spiraled down spiritually. God sent prophets to warn the people of coming judgment if they did not turn back, but the people did not heed the warnings. So just as God had promised, He removed His people from the land because of their idolatry. But God did not abandon them during their exile. As prophesied, God's people returned to their land. However, their hearts were still not fully committed to Him, thus the need for the coming Messiah.

 WHERE WE'VE BEEN: EXILE AND RETURN

Solomon takes foreign wives and allows their foreign gods to clutter the land. His son continues the line of rulers and the kingdom is divided into the Northern Kingdom (Israel) and the Southern Kingdom (Judah). Prophets confront the people but they persist in their idolatry. The Northern Kingdom falls to Assyria and the Southern Kingdom is carried away into Babylonian captivity. When they are freed, they return to a nation and kingdom far less glorious than before and are still unable to keep their promises.

 WHERE WE'RE HEADED: JESUS

A descendant of Adam, Abraham, and David, Jesus is the One who crushes the head of Satan, will bless all nations, and reigns forever. Jesus, the God-Man, enters humanity through the womb of a virgin, perfectly obeys the law that we could never obey, dies as the once-and-for-all sacrifice for our sins, and rises from the dead, conquering Satan, sin, and death. He inaugurates His eternal kingdom and secures salvation for His people.

Elijah & the Gods

Read 1 Kings 18.

This passage tells an incredible story that highlights the difference between God and the gods that the people were tempted to worship. Elijah, a prophet of God, issued a challenge to 450 prophets of a false, little-g god named Baal. Elijah issued the challenge: "Let's find out whose god is God. You pray to your god, to Baal. I will pray to my God, Yahweh, the self-existing One. The god who answers by fire is really God. You guys go first."

So the 450 prophets of Baal danced around the fire for hours. They cut themselves, screamed, worshiped, and begged their god to light the altar on fire. "Baal, answer us!"

Elijah threw down some ancient smack talk. "Shout a little louder," he cried. "Maybe your god is sleeping. I wonder why he cannot hear you?"

But there was no sound. No one answered. No one paid attention.

Then, Elijah stepped up and asked for water to be poured all over the altar because He knew what would happen. He knew that his God hears, and his God answers. Elijah asked for more water to be put on the altar so it would be clear that God is the One who sent the fire. No one would be able to say that the fire happened because two rocks rubbed together and created a spark or the sun caught a blade of grass on fire. The water was added so it would be absolutely clear that God had answered. After Elijah prayed, fire came from heaven, consumed the altar, and licked up all the water on the ground.

Our God hears. Elijah wanted the people to understand how foolish it is to worship idols that cannot hear and gods that are powerless. Sadly, the people as a whole, even after this moment, continued to worship and pursue gods rather than the one true God.

The things of this life we are tempted to pursue are powerless to save us, too. They are powerless to give us true life. God is the only One who can answer with fire.

What are some things of the world that you have foolishly pursued?

What was the result of your pursuit?

How have you seen God do things in your life that only He could do?

What's keeping you from whole-heartedly pursuing Him now?

DAY TWO

Daniel

Some people see living in America as living in a Christian nation, perhaps similar to the state of the nation of Israel during King David's reign. Under David's leadership, the people feared God and were united. But if you want to make a comparison between life as believers in the United States and life in the Old Testament for God's people, a more accurate comparison would be the period of Israel's Babylonian captivity. Like that time period, we are living in a time that is becoming more and more secular and more and more tolerant of everything—of everything except people who insist that their belief system is absolute. So how should we live? Daniel's friends provide an example.

Daniel 3 tells the story of Shadrach, Meshach, and Abednego, but these were not their real names. The king of Babylon, Nebuchadnezzar, had besieged Jerusalem, taken the people into captivity, and given them new names and new jobs. Shadrach, Meshach, and Abednego tolerated the new jobs and new names, trusting God's plan for them in a new culture. But in Daniel 3, the king asked them to do something they were unwilling to do. He announced that every person must bow down and worship a 90-foot gold statue that he had erected. He set up an orchestra and told the people that as soon as the music started, they must bow down to worship the image. Anyone who did not worship the image would be cast into a fiery furnace. The temptation presented to the three Israelite young men was not to stop worshiping God, but to worship the king's god, too.

How do we face a similar temptation? Explain.

The idols of this world aren't asking us to give up our worship of God, just add them to the mix. But because God is the only true God, He says we must only worship Him.

Shadrach, Meshach, and Abednego refused to bow. King Nebuchadnezzar was furious, scolded them, and offered them another chance. They let him know that they, of course, did not need a second opportunity. They believed that God was able to rescue them, but if He chose not to, they still would not bow. What faith! So Nebuchadnezzar threw them into the furnace, a furnace so hot that it killed the soldiers who threw them in.

Read Daniel 3:24-30.

Was it Christ who jumped in the fire with them? We're not sure. Theologians have debated whether this was Christ (who has always existed) or an angel. Regardless, after pulling the guys from the furnace, Nebuchadnezzar admitted, "There is no other god who is able to deliver like this" (Dan. 3:29).

In the pagan Babylonian culture, Shadrach, Meshach, and Abednego were willing to work new jobs and take new names. But they were not willing to bow to another god.

When the prophet Jeremiah wrote to God's people living in Babylon, he instructed them to build houses, plant gardens, live, and to even pray for the welfare of Babylon (Jer. 29:4-7). So living in Babylon, based on God's instructions, meant caring for people there and seeking the welfare of the city. But it also meant not compromising their commitment to God.

God put you in your career, your job, and your neighborhood. Live there. Pray for the people God has surrounded you with. Work hard. Do all you can for the welfare of those around you. As you do so, only bow to Him.

In what ways are you tempted to bow down to other gods? Explain.

DAY THREE
God In the Story of Esther

*A king's heart is like channeled water in the LORD's hand:
He directs it wherever he chooses.*
Proverbs 21:1

The Book of Esther does not mention God by name. But since God is the center of the Bible's story, how can there be a book that does not mention His name? Some say His name is intentionally not used in the book to show that He is still in charge, even when we don't see Him. Regardless, in the Book of Esther, we learn that we must not mistake God's silence for His absence. Often, He is working behind-the-scenes, directing events and implementing His plans.

In the timeline, the story of Esther occurs after God's people have been taken into Babylonian captivity. The Persians conquered the Babylonians and set the Jews free to return home. But many stayed, continuing to live in a land that was not their own, under the rule of a Persian king. The Book of Esther opens with a massive feast held by the Persian king Xerxes. He threw a 180-day party concluding with a seven-day feast. Everyone was drunk, and Xerxes decided to show off his pretty wife, Vashti. He sent for her to come wearing her crown, to show off her beauty.

She refused. The king was livid, and his counselors advised him to divorce his wife and ban her from his presence. After all he was king, and no one could treat him that way. The whole point of the feast was to show off his power, yet he did not have power over his own wife. So he banned Vashti, his wife, from his presence, and launched a search throughout the royal provinces for a new queen.

Mordecai and his beautiful cousin Esther lived in one of the provinces. When Esther's parents died, Mordecai adopted her as his own daughter. During the search for a queen, she was taken into Xerxes' harem where other virgins were preparing to go before the king. Each day, Mordecai walked by the court where Esther stayed and talked with her. He encouraged her to conceal her nationality and family background as she hoped to be the next queen of Persia. Eventually Esther was summoned before the king, and he was blown away with her beauty. He loved her more than any of the others and made her his queen.

The Story of God

After Esther became queen, Mordecai happened to overhear a plot to assassinate the king. Mordecai told Esther who then told Xerxes, giving due credit to Mordecai. Mordecai had saved the king, but his reward was overlooked.

At this point in the story, a new character is introduced: Haman. He was promoted to a high position, right at the place in the story where we would expect to find a report of Mordecai's promotion. This turn of events does not seem fair. Haman was promoted and not Mordecai? What is going on here? All the officials bowed down and paid honor to Haman except Mordecai. This infuriated Haman, and he devised a plan to destroy not only Mordecai, but all the Jews.

Esther had been queen for five years when Haman reported to the king that a certain ethnic group (the Jews) did not obey the king's laws. He told the king that it was not in the king's best interest to tolerate such behavior and that this group should be eliminated. Xerxes gave Haman full authority to do as he pleased, and Haman moved forward with his plan. He drew up the order in the first month of the year that instructed the officials in all the provinces to annihilate the Jews in the last month of the year. When Mordecai heard the news, he mourned in sackcloth and ashes.

After Esther tried to get him to cease his mourning, Mordecai sent word to her about what was happening, with a command for her to go to the king. He told her to seek the king's favor and plead for her people. This frightened Esther. She sent word back to Mordecai explaining that she no longer routinely saw Xerxes, which was likely typical for a king with many concubines. She couldn't go to the king uninvited without risking her life. Unless he extended his scepter as a sign of grace, she would be killed on the spot. Mordecai told her that she would face death regardless, and that perhaps she had been placed in this position "for such a time as this" (Esth. 4:14).

To save her people, Esther had to risk her life before the king and before Haman. She requested that Mordecai have everyone fast for her before she made her appearance. When she walked into the king's presence, he accepted her and offered her anything she wanted up to half the kingdom. She simply asked for he and Haman to attend a banquet. In the meantime, Haman had built massive gallows on which to hang Mordecai because he still refused to bow before Haman.

At the first banquet, Esther did not reveal her request, but at the second one she told the king that she and her people were to be killed. Xerxes' honor was offended that someone would make such plans. When he found out Haman devised the plan and used his authority for the decree, he walked out of the room in a rage. The gallows Haman had built for Mordecai were used on Haman. And because Haman was executed as a traitor, his property was confiscated and given to Esther.

Week 6: Jesus

The king's signet ring which had previously been given to Haman was given to Mordecai. The ring vested Mordecai with the power and authority previously given to Haman. The former heinous decree could not be dismissed, but Esther and Mordecai were given power and authority to write another one to counteract Haman's decree. They decreed that Jews could take whatever measures were necessary to defend themselves. In the armed conflict, the Jews struck down those who hated them. They were victorious.

This fight was the foundation of Purim, a Jewish holiday that exists to this day.

Passover celebrates the deliverance of the Jews through extraordinary events. Purim celebrates the survival of the Jews through ordinary events.

The author of Esther was teaching God's people that sometimes God quietly works behind the scenes for their benefit. The Passover remembers a time when God delivered His people from Egyptian captivity through very visible and awe-inspiring miracles such as the plagues. In Esther, God is the silent yet sovereign King, orchestrating events and working behind the scenes to rescue His people.

God is working in the ordinary details of your life, too. He is still the sovereign King using great and small things to accomplish His purposes.

How have you seen God work behind the scenes in your ordinary life?

Week 6: Jesus

Malachi & Your Worship

Malachi is a "post-exilic" prophet (along with Haggai and Zechariah), meaning he was a messenger to God's people after they returned from Babylonian exile. While the people had returned and were worshiping God again, their worship was out of duty rather than delight. The priests were offering God leftover animals and not bringing their best to Him.

Read Malachi 1:6-14.

According to Leviticus 22, priests were to only bring pure and unblemished animals to sacrifice to God. But now, the priests were offering God blind and diseased animals. God essentially said that their employer (their governor) would fire them if they had offered him what they were offering God. God preferred no offering in comparison to a half-hearted, going-through-the-motions type of offering.

Some struggle with God's insistence on being worshiped, as if this makes God like the insecure guy at the office who constantly fights for attention. But the guy at the office acts that way because he is deficient in his character. There is nothing deficient in God's character. He passionately pursues His own worship because there is nothing greater for Him to pursue. Three thoughts to consider:

GOD MUST BE WORSHIPED.
Notice Malachi 1:11. God's name will be great among the nations. God was declaring that He would find worshipers from every nation. And He does.

Christ was sacrificed to rescue people from every tribe, tongue, and nation. He pursues worshipers from outside of Israel—including you! And He is always worshiped. When you slept last night, someone on the other side of the world was worshiping.

If God did not desire and demand worship, He would not be God. If there were something more excellent, more beautiful, and more praiseworthy than God, then that thing would be God. But there is nothing better, nothing more amazing than Him. He stands alone.

WE WILL WORSHIP.
The people God was addressing hadn't stopped worshiping; they had just stopped worshiping Him. They viewed something else as greater than God. Maybe they longed for comfort and wanted the best meat for themselves. Perhaps security was their god, offering God the cheap lambs so they could sell the better ones to get more money. You don't have to be taught to worship. You are always giving value and worth to something or someone. But God alone is Master and Father, and anything else we worship is less than Him.

THUS, HIS COMMANDS TO WORSHIP HIM ARE GRACIOUS INVITATIONS.
These words in Malachi are very strong. But when we understand that God must be worshiped and we must worship, we realize that God pursuing our worship is good for us. His commands to worship Him are gracious invitations because He is commanding us to find ultimate joy.

The Old Testament ends during this period of time. Nehemiah rebuilt the wall, but the people could not keep their commitments. The exiles were back in the land but were now offering God leftover sacrifices. While some have been faithful, the overarching trend of God's people was a failure to worship God alone. They needed a Rescuer. So do we. Malachi prophesied that the Rescuer is coming.

See, I am going to send my messenger, and he will clear the way before me. Then the Lord you seek will suddenly come to his temple, the Messenger of the covenant you delight in—see, he is coming," says the LORD of Armies.
Malachi 3:1

The messenger who clears the way will be John the Baptist. Christ is the Messenger of the new covenant—a new promise that will include people from every nation.

He is also the mediator of the new covenant as He brings us to Himself through His death on the cross. The Old Testament ends with people desperate for the One who will change our disobedient hearts. The Old Testament ends with a longing for a new King, a better King.

Do you find yourself worshiping and serving God out of duty or delight? Explain.

REFLECT

 Before attending the group session, look back over the timeline and four days of personal study. Use this space to write down any thoughts, questions, or prayers related to redemptive history and the Bible's one overarching story.

GROUP SESSION

WEEK 6

Jesus

In this week's time together, we reach the story's climactic peak—everything has been leading to Jesus. The plot twist that nobody fully anticipated had been written into the story from the beginning. A descendant of Adam, Abraham, and David, Jesus is the One who crushes the head of Satan, will bless all nations, and reigns forever. Jesus, the God-Man, enters humanity through the womb of a virgin, perfectly obeys the law that we could never obey, dies as the once-and-for-all sacrifice for our sins, and rises from the dead, conquering Satan, sin, and death. He inaugurates His eternal kingdom and secures salvation for His people.

 Open your time together in prayer, asking God to help you understand and apply the truth revealed in His Word.

LEADERS: Sign in to the Rooted Network Digital Hub and stream this week's teaching video.

EVERYONE: Use the following pages for notes and group discussion.

Week 6 Teaching Outline

What the Gospels reveal about Jesus:

1. The King has arrived.

2. His kingdom is announced.

3. His kingdom is upside down.

4. The King serves and suffers.

5. The King conquers.

How the Bible's story points to Jesus:

1. Jesus is greater than Adam.

2. Jesus is greater than Abraham.

3. Jesus is greater than Moses.

4. Jesus is greater than Joshua.

5. Jesus is greater than David.

6. Jesus is greater than all the prophets.

NOTES

Discussion Guide

1. Share a quick summary of highlights from Weeks 1–5. Why is this week an important point in redemptive history and the unfolding story of God?

2. How does the introduction of Jesus differ in the four Gospels? Why are these differences important for us today?

3. Eric pointed out five things the Gospels reveal about Jesus. How might your understanding of the "good news" change if something was left out?

4. What does the phrase "kingdom of God" mean?

5. How do Jesus' miracles point to the kingdom of God?

6. What did Eric mean when he said that Jesus' kingdom is an upside-down kingdom? Explain.

Read Matthew 18:3 aloud.

**3 "Truly I tell you," he said, "unless you turn and become like little children, you will never enter the kingdom of heaven."
Matthew 18:3**

7. Why do we have to become like children to enter the kingdom of God? Why is this difficult for some of us?

8. How do people misunderstand the sacrifice of Jesus? Why is the cross so offensive to some?

9. How would you explain that the whole story of the Old Testament points to Jesus?

10. How can a person's heart be changed? Explain.

Look back over the personal study.

11. What was especially meaningful or helpful in understanding the story of God and your life with Christ?

    Day 1: Elijah & the Gods

    Day 2: Daniel

    Day 3: God In the Story of Esther

    Day 4: Malachi & Your Worship

    Day 5: Reflection

12. How does the takeaway affect your view of Scripture? How will you respond to this part of the story?

> Takeaway:
> **We have hope because Jesus cares about our hearts, taking away sin and shame.**

WEEK 7

PERSONAL BIBLE STUDY

Our Session 6 teaching focused on Jesus, the King who has come to serve and save. We discussed how His kingdom is not like an earthly kingdom but is totally turned upside down. We also reinforced the truth that all of Scripture points to Jesus. The story is about Him. In your personal study this week, you'll examine an account of Jesus making that point Himself. You'll also learn more about Jesus' kingdom and who is fit for it.

WHERE WE'VE BEEN: JESUS

A descendant of Adam, Abraham, and David, Jesus is the One who crushes the head of Satan, will bless all nations, and reigns forever. Jesus, the God-Man, enters humanity through the womb of a virgin, perfectly obeys the law that we could never obey, dies as the once-and-for-all sacrifice for our sins, and rises from the dead, conquering Satan, sin, and death. He inaugurates His eternal kingdom and secures salvation for His people.

WHERE WE'RE HEADED: A NEW PEOPLE

After His ascension to heaven, Jesus sends the promised Holy Spirit and His disciples turn the world upside down preaching the good news of Jesus. This good news is known as the gospel. In the midst of intense persecution, the gospel spreads, and Gentiles and Jews form a new people. Churches are planted in cities, and apostles write letters encouraging and instructing the people in the grace of Christ and their response to His grace.

Week 7: A New People

DAY ONE
The First Easter Sermon

Fittingly, Jesus was the first to preach an Easter sermon. Not only did He conquer the grave, but He also pursued people immediately after doing so to ensure they understood the reality of His resurrection. His first message was heard by two guys who were walking the seven miles from Jerusalem to Emmaus. As Jesus began walking along with them, He asked what they were talking about. One of the men, Cleopas, responded with a hint of sarcasm: "Are you the only visitor in Jerusalem who doesn't know …?" (Luke 24:18). They then shared the news that the Jesus of Nazareth, who had performed miracles, wowed crowds, and spoken with incredible authority had been crucified. They were deeply disappointed because they had hoped Jesus was the one to rescue Israel. They were also troubled by reports that angels were declaring Jesus was alive. It was a lot to process and take in. Jesus rebuked them for their weak faith.

He said to them, "How foolish you are, and how slow to believe all that the prophets have spoken! Wasn't it necessary for the Messiah to suffer these things and enter into his glory?" Then beginning with Moses and all the Prophets, he interpreted for them the things concerning himself in all the Scriptures.
Luke 24:25-27

Jesus then showed them how all the Scripture points to Him. They didn't recognize Him until after he had blessed, broken, and given them bread. Jesus then disappeared. The two men hurried back to Jerusalem to find the disciples. As they were sharing how Jesus found them on the road and preached His own Easter sermon, Jesus appeared to the whole group.
He told them, "These are my words that I spoke to you while I was still with you—that everything written about me in the Law of Moses, the Prophets, and the Psalms must be fulfilled." Then he opened their minds to understand the Scriptures. He also said to them, "This is what is written: The Messiah will suffer and rise from the dead the third day, and repentance for forgiveness of sins would be proclaimed in his name to all the nations, beginning at Jerusalem."
Luke 24:44-47

For the Jews, the Law, the Prophets, and the Psalms were their entire Bible. Therefore, Jesus was essentially saying, "All that you have read and studied points to Me!" In the Law, God gave His people commands and set up a priest and sacrificial system because of man's inability to keep the commands. In the Prophets, God spoke through men to call His people to truth, justice, and faithfulness. In Psalms, God's people celebrated the rule of God. Many of the psalms were written by David, the king who, though deeply flawed, united the people and ruled them skillfully. Because Jesus is the point of all the Scripture, we see that He is the perfect Priest, the perfect Prophet, and the perfect King.

JESUS IS THE PERFECT PRIEST (THE LAW).

While priests in the Old Testament needed to offer sacrifices every single day, Jesus offered Himself for our sins "once for all" (Heb. 7:27). On the cross He yelled out, "It is finished" (John 19:30) because the full payment for our sins was paid, and the wrath of God was quenched. Other priests offered animals as sacrifices, but Christ offered Himself as the pure and perfect sacrifice—the sacrifice to end all other sacrifices.

JESUS IS THE PERFECT PROPHET (THE PROPHETS).

The prophets confronted people in their sin and called the people to repentance. Jesus likewise called people to repentance but also called them to Himself. "Repent" and "Come to Me" were messages He heralded. Jesus is full of both truth and grace. He is also the Prophet to whom all other prophets pointed.

JESUS IS THE PERFECT KING (THE PSALMS).

Every other king, even the good ones, fell woefully short of God's greatness and grace. Jesus stands alone as the King of kings. King David wrote of the Faithful One who would not see decay in Psalm 16:

Therefore my heart is glad
and my spirit rejoices;
my body also rests securely.
For you will not abandon me to Sheol;
you will not allow your faithful one to see decay.
Psalm 16:9-10

Clearly David was not speaking of himself because David's body did see decay. But King Jesus' body never did. Not only did He preach His own Easter sermon, He rose from the grave before He did! He is the King who rules and reigns forever.

Jesus is your perfect Priest, Prophet, and King.

What does it mean for you that Jesus is your Priest?

What does it mean for you that Jesus is your Prophet?

What does it mean for you that Jesus is your King?

DAY TWO
The Kingdom & the Birds of the Sky

As we talked about in our group session, Jesus announced the good news of His kingdom. He is the King who rules and reigns forever, and we are invited into His kingdom! Jesus also taught about the kingdom of heaven through parables. In Matthew 13, He offered six parables about His kingdom. Let's look at one of those parables today:

He presented another parable to them: "The kingdom of heaven is like a mustard seed that a man took and sowed in his field. It's the smallest of all the seeds, but when grown, it's taller than the garden plants and becomes a tree, so that the birds of the sky come and nest in its branches."
Matthew 13:31-32

When Jesus said the kingdom of heaven is like a tiny mustard seed, perhaps the crowd understood that the kingdom of heaven on this earth would start small. And it did. For the most part, Christ's arrival on this earth was a minor and unnoticed event to the vast majority of humanity. It was not broadcast on FOX or CNN. There were no marketing plans and no campaign offices set up to let people know that a new leader was arriving. On the night of Christ's birth, no one even provided Joseph and Mary a room. So Jesus was placed in a manger, a feeding trough for livestock.

After His birth, He grew up in a backwoods town in Galilee, far from the influence and affluence of the Roman Empire. When Jesus was around 30, He began teaching publicly and performing miracles. He invited 12 disciples to live with Him and follow Him. These 12 disciples were normal guys, uneducated, not from the religious elite, rough around the edges, and impulsive. After Jesus died, rose from the dead, and ascended back to heaven, about 120 people gathered together in prayer in Jerusalem waiting for direction from the Holy Spirit on what to do next. The kingdom of heaven started small.

But Jesus assured His disciples the kingdom would not stay small. It would grow and become like a tree. In Israel, the mustard plant would grow to be as tall as 15 feet high. It was a garden plant, but the largest garden plant; so large that some would refer to it as a tree. Like the mustard plant, the kingdom of heaven in this world has grown very large. The rule of God has expanded to people all over the globe. The kingdom is still expanding and will continue to expand, including people from every tribe, tongue, and nation.

Even as you are doing this study, there are millions of other men, women, and children around the world studying the Bible. Some do so in secret because it is illegal to be a Christian and their lives are in constant danger. Some are meeting under trees in remote villages because they have no space under roof. But today in many different languages and dialects, Christ is being praised and glorified and the kingdom of heaven is expanding. What Jesus said would happen has happened and continues to happen.

But that is not all Jesus was saying in this parable. The kingdom grows to a large tree "so that the birds of the sky come and nest in its branches" (v.32). What does this mean? This phrase took the listeners back to several Old Testament passages describing earthly kingdoms that were so powerful and fruitful that people outside of those kingdoms benefited from them. When Israel was in Babylonian captivity under Nebuchadnezzar, Daniel interpreted the ruler's dream. In Nebuchadnezzar's dream, he saw the following:

The tree grew large and strong;
its top reached to the sky,
and it was visible to the ends of the earth.
Its leaves were beautiful, its fruit was abundant,
and on it was food for all.
Wild animals found shelter under it,
the birds of the air lived in its branches,
and every creature was fed from it.
Daniel 4:11-12

Daniel told the king of Babylon, "That tree is you" (Dan. 4:22). The Babylonian kingdom was so fruitful that the culture, education, architecture, and philosophy of other nations was impacted by its influence. The crowd also knew of the Assyrian kingdom. When the Assyrian kingdom was prospering, the "birds of the sky nested in its branches" (Ezek. 31:6). Both Babylonian and Assyrian kingdoms impacted outsiders.

And so it is with the kingdom of heaven. The kingdom of heaven influences people outside of the kingdom. If you live under the rule of God, people at your work and in your neighborhood benefit from your influence. As you walk with integrity, work hard, love and forgive people, and bring your best to your craft, you bless and influence others. You are a part of a people that blesses all other peoples. And as we influence the world around us, we are commanded to invite others into His kingdom. We are commanded to make disciples, urging others to receive His forgiveness and to live with Jesus as their King.

While the Babylonian, Assyrian, and other kingdoms rose and fell, the kingdom of heaven will never end. Our King eternally reigns!

How have you seen your church influence people outside the kingdom of heaven? How are you and your family doing that? Be specific.

DAY THREE
Kingdom Man: A Pharisee or a Tax Collector

The people who are fit for the kingdom of God, the kingdom that Jesus inaugurated, are not the strong, the proud, or other type people you might expect. To enter His kingdom, we must become humble like children. To enter His kingdom, we must embrace our weakness and fragility and realize how desperately we need Him. Jesus told a parable about a Pharisee and a tax collector. One was qualified for His kingdom and the other was not. Jesus shocked the crowd when He revealed who was justified and right with God.

Pharisees were religious and devout individuals. The word Pharisee means "the separated ones," stemming from their desire to live separate and distinct lives, lives that were holy and pure. They fasted twice a week. They tithed. They prayed regularly. They were serious about their faith. Mothers wanted their children to be Pharisees.

Tax collectors were polar opposite of the Pharisees. They were known as traitors because they worked for Rome, the foreign invaders who occupied the land. They were also seen as thieves, hiking up rates to line their own pockets. They were despised. So when Jesus wanted to make a point to the religious people about not trusting in their own works, He told a story about a Pharisee and a tax collector.

We often think about humanity in terms of good people and bad people. Some would think that if a story's main characters are a Pharisee and a tax collector, this story is going to be about a good, religious man and a bad, sinful one. But Jesus looks at humanity in different terms. We are all bad, all of us. There is no one righteous, no not one. He views us in terms of humble and proud.

Read Luke 18:9-14.

The Pharisee celebrated his own goodness. Even though he addressed God, he really prayed to himself about himself. He listed all the things that he was not. "I am so glad I am not greedy. I am not unrighteous. I am not an adulterer like other people I know. And I am not like this tax collector who steals money from others." He then listed some of the things he did. "I fast. I give. And look at me right now, I am praying." Yet for all that activity, this Pharisee never really encountered the Lord. Because when we encounter the Lord, we declare how great He is, not how great we are.

The Pharisee looked down on others because of his pride in all he was doing for God. Anytime we think we are righteous in our own goodness, we will immediately look down on others. We will consider ourselves a special kind of Christian, at a level to which others have not arrived. But we can't bring our spiritual résumé to Christ in pride. If we attempt to stand before Him in our own goodness, we insult Him, saying we believe His death was in vain.

The tax collector's prayer was very different from the Pharisee's. The tax collector mourned his own sinfulness. He would not even look up to heaven. He prayed, "Turn Your wrath from me" (v.13). The language here is powerful. When he begged God for mercy, he used the word *hilaskomai*, which is translated *propitiation*. It is a powerful word that is used several times in the New Testament. It is the same word used to describe the mercy seat on top of the ark of covenant.

Remember that the scene for Jesus' parable is the temple. Inside the temple was the Most Holy Place where the high priest would enter once a year to make atonement for the sins of the people. Before entering, the high priest would take a goat and sacrifice it on the altar in the outer court of the temple. He would take the blood from the goat and bring it into the Most Holy Place, then sprinkle it on the seat of propitiation, also called the mercy seat, which served as the lid of the ark of the covenant. Inside the ark of the covenant were the Ten Commandments, the commandments that bring condemnation because we are unable to live up to them. The blood being sprinkled on the seat of propitiation signified that God's wrath was being appeased. It was turned from His people and placed instead on the goat that was sacrificed. The goat received the punishment instead of the people.

In Jesus' story, the tax collector understands this truth. He is outside the temple, hearing the sacrifices being made and saying, "God, let those sacrifices bear the punishment for my sin. I know that because You are holy, You can't just forget my sin. It has to be punished. Please God, turn Your wrath for my sin away from me."

The tax collector mourned his own sinfulness, and he went home justified.

The word *justified* means he went home in complete right standing with God. The tax collector did not merely go home with his sins forgotten; he went home right with God. He went home with the perfection of God applied to His life. He went home as if he had never stolen, never lied, never cheated, always done the right thing, always treated people the right way, always been loving and gracious. He went home as if he had obeyed at all times every one of the commandments that were sealed in the ark of the covenant. He went home right with God not because he, in his own merit, actually lived those commandments but because God had justified Him.

Those who are justified realize they are weak before God, in need of His mercy and grace, and call out to Him in faith. Others who are like the Pharisee are prideful and full of themselves. In reality, they are people who are empty.

Do you identify more with the Pharisee or the tax collector? Why?

DAY FOUR
Miracle of Bread

The miracles Jesus performed proved He is the eternal King. When John the Baptist sent people to ask Jesus if He was the One, Jesus sent word back that the sick are healed, the dead raised, and the blind receive sight. The miracles supported His claims to deity. The only miracle recorded in all four Gospel accounts is the miracle of Jesus feeding 5,000 men (when you include the women and children, the crowd would have been much larger).

Read John 6:1-14 and John 6:22-35.

Jesus made several famous "I AM" statements in the Gospel of John. His declaration "I am the bread of life" was the first (v. 35).

When Jesus declared Himself to be "I AM," He was declaring Himself to be God. As we learned earlier, long before Jesus walked the earth, God spoke to Moses from a burning bush, calling him to lead God's people out of Egyptian slavery to freedom. When Moses asked God what His name was, God replied, "I AM WHO I AM" (Ex. 3:14). So when Jesus referred to Himself as I AM, He was declaring Himself to be the One who spoke to Moses from the bush, the One who is from the beginning, the One who is God.

Later in the Gospel of John, Jesus shocked and infuriated the crowd by saying, "Before Abraham, I am" (John 8:58). He was declaring His eternal nature—that He was before Abraham, and that He has always been. The crowd attempted to stone Him to death because they viewed His statement as blasphemy, and the punishment for blasphemy was stoning. Jesus was either guilty of blasphemy, or He is indeed God.

Of course, anyone can claim to be God. You may have a crazy uncle who talks a big game at the annual family gathering or a cousin who is always story-topping you with some tale about something great he pulled off. Anyone can claim anything.

But Jesus did much more than just claim to be God. He backed it up.

When Jesus declared, "I am the resurrection and the life," He raised Lazarus from the dead (John 11:25). When Jesus declared, "I am the light of the world," He put light into a blind man's eyes (John 9:5). And before Jesus declared "I am the bread of life," He fed 5,000 men with two fish and five bread loaves (John 6:35). No one but Jesus can pull that off.

The crowd knew the story of Moses and the "bread from heaven." After their ancestors were freed from Egypt, they wandered in the desert before entering the promised land. During that time, God fed His people by providing manna from heaven.

Jesus told the crowd that in Him, God was now giving them the true bread from heaven. Jesus is better. He is the eternal bread from heaven, the One who came to sustain us and satisfy our souls. When we receive Him, when we feast on Him, we are never hungry again (John 6:35). Your job, your friends or family, your career goals, your dream house or boat cannot and will not quench you. Only Jesus can. Only He is the Bread of life.

How is your life different when Jesus is the One who sustains and satisfies you?

What's your biggest hindrance in allowing Jesus to do that?

REFLECT

Before attending the group session, look back over the timeline and four days of personal study. Use this space to write down any thoughts, questions, or prayers related to redemptive history and the Bible's one overarching story.

GROUP SESSION

WEEK 7

A New People

In this week's time together, the story of God continues as we see the result of history's greatest Hero and most dramatic rescue. After His ascension to heaven, Jesus sends the promised Holy Spirit and His disciples turn the world upside down preaching the good news of Jesus. This time, God's people experience a season of incredible faithfulness. In the midst of intense persecution, the gospel spreads, and Gentiles and Jews form a new people. Churches are planted in cities, and apostles write letters encouraging and instructing the people in the grace of Christ and their response to His grace.

 Open your time together in prayer, asking God to help you understand and apply the truth revealed in His Word.

LEADERS: Sign in to the Rooted Network Digital Hub and stream this week's teaching video.

EVERYONE: Use the following pages for notes and group discussion.

Week 7 Teaching Outline

The people of God live in an "already-but-not-yet" kingdom.

Apostles wrote letters to churches—people like you and me.

Most letters start with belief and move to behavior.

Who are we as the Church? Three things about our new identity:

1. We are a new people.

The Christian faith is radically exclusive and radically inclusive.

2. We have new power.

God's Spirit has moved into our lives.

3. We are on a holy mission.

People are going to be rescued from every tribe, tongue, and nation.

There is no greater mission than to take the gospel to other people.

NOTES

Discussion Guide

1. Share a quick summary of highlights from Weeks 1–6. Why is this week an important point in redemptive history and the unfolding story of God?

1. What does it mean that Jesus' kingdom is "already, but not yet"? Explain.

2. How does understanding the kingdom is "already, but not yet" help you deal with the difficulties of life?

3. How would you explain the great exchange?

4. What does it mean to be clothed in Christ's righteousness?

Read the following scripture aloud.

17 He came and proclaimed the good news of peace to you who were far away and peace to those who were near. 18 For through him we both have access in one Spirit to the Father. 19 So, then, you are no longer foreigners and strangers, but fellow citizens with the saints, and members of God's household, 20 built on the foundation of the apostles and prophets, with Christ Jesus himself as the cornerstone. 21 In him the whole building, being put together, grows into a holy temple in the Lord. 22 In him you are also being built together for God's dwelling in the Spirit.
Ephesians 2:17–22

5. What does it mean for Jesus to be your cornerstone? Is He? Why or why not? Does everything in your life revolve around Jesus? Explain.

6. Eric said the Holy Spirit has moved into our lives and now we can become more like Jesus. Are you more like Jesus today than you were last week? Last year? Why or why not? What does your answer reveal about being a disciple and making disciples?

Look up Matthew 28:18–20 and Acts 1:8. Read it aloud.

7. How are you currently carrying out Jesus' mission to reconcile people from every tribe, tongue, and nation? Honestly, what other "missions" in your life appear to be more important? How can Jesus' mission become the priority, even in your normal daily responsibilities and interests?

Look back over the personal study.

8. What was especially meaningful or helpful in understanding the story of God and your life with Christ?

    📕 Day 1: The First Easter Sermon

    📕 Day 2: The Kingdom & the Birds of the Sky

    📕 Day 3: Kingdom Man: A Pharisee or a Tax Collector

    📕 Day 4: Miracle of Bread

    📕 Day 5: Reflection

9. How does the takeaway affect your view of Scripture? How will you respond to this part of the story?

10. Think through your story of transformation and spiritual growth for next week. Consider how your life-changing experience with Jesus relates to being a part of His new people.

> **Takeaway:**
> **We are God's people, filled with the Holy Spirit to be His witnesses, making disciples of all nations.**

Week 7: A New People

WEEK 8

DAY ONE
Christ Is Above All

Your perspective on what is ultimate or supreme will deeply impact how you order your life. In Paul's letter to the Colossians, he made clear who he viewed as supreme. He wrote, "All things have been created through Him and for Him . . . and by Him all things hold together" (Col. 1:16).

Sometime between AD 161 and 180, Marcus Aurelius wrote his famous Meditations. Some believe Marcus Aurelius was a great leader, a great emperor. He is portrayed favorably, for example, in the movie *Gladiator* as the elderly leader whom Russell Crowe loves and admires. We also know, from history, that persecution of Christians escalated under his rule. He either directed or allowed the torture and death of believers. In his classic work, Meditations, Marcus Aurelius wrote: "Nature. All things come of you, have their being in you, and return to you."[11]

Clearly, the apostle Paul and Marcus Aurelius held two very different perspectives on what is ultimate. Marcus Aurelius' perspective was that nature is supreme—that what we can taste, touch, see, and smell is where we find our meaning. Many men live as if they believe what Aurelius wrote, searching for meaning and identity in nature, in the things of this world. The Christian perspective is very different, though. We believe that the one God, who created all things, is ultimate and we find meaning and significance in Him. And we believe that Jesus the Christ is God.

In many letters in the New Testament, the apostles devoted time to teaching who Jesus is and to correcting false teaching and beliefs about Him. In the following incredible passage, the apostle Paul reminded his readers and us that Jesus is above all.

Read Colossians 1:15-20.

HE IS THE IMAGE OF THE INVISIBLE GOD,
God created us in the image of God, but we are not the image of the invisible God. Jesus is different. He is not created in the image of God because He is not created; He is the image of God.

Remember the second commandment in the Ten Commandments? (See Ex. 20:4-5.) One of the reasons God was so adamant to His people not to make any image of Him was because every image we create falls woefully short of the reality of who God is. But Jesus is different. He is not a created image. He does not fall woefully short. He is the image of God.

THE FIRSTBORN OVER ALL CREATION.

The word, *firstborn*, in the original language refers primarily to position or rank, not chronology. The firstborn son, in this culture, was given authority and rank from the father. The firstborn would receive the inheritance. Jesus is the firstborn. He is first in rank, position, and authority, and He has received all that is the Father's.

FOR EVERYTHING WAS CREATED BY HIM,

Jesus did not come into existence when He was born into this world. He has always existed. He was not only present in creation, He created the whole world and everything in it. He created the great foods we eat, the beaches we enjoy, the sunset and sunrise we observe. He created Mary, His earthly mother, and He created the trees, which formed the cross He would embrace. Everything was created by Him.

IN HEAVEN AND ON EARTH, THE VISIBLE AND THE INVISIBLE, WHETHER THRONES OR DOMINIONS OR RULERS OR AUTHORITIES.

The language of "thrones or dominions or ruler or authorities" is used elsewhere in the Scripture, and it describes evil supernatural powers that we do not see. In Ephesians 6:12, Paul wrote that "our battle is not against flesh and blood, but against the rulers, against the authorities, ... against the spiritual forces of evil in the heavens." God created them too. He created all things, even the evil spirits that seek to deceive and destroy. But understand this: the demons were not created evil; they became evil. They sinned against God and were cast from His presence. In the same way, there are good things that God has created that we distort and ruin in our sinfulness. But this does not change the reality that He has created everything.

ALL THINGS HAVE BEEN CREATED THROUGH HIM AND FOR HIM.

Not only has Christ created all things, but also all things have been created for Him. All things have been created to bring Him glory. He created the sunset and the sky so we can see visibly the creativity of our invisible God. He created the food we enjoy so when we taste it we might say, "Wow, God is really good to us."

He created all things so that all things could bring Him glory. One day even the demons will bow to Him and declare He is God.

HE IS BEFORE ALL THINGS, AND BY HIM ALL THINGS HOLD TOGETHER.

Marcus Aurelius said that all things have their being in nature. However, the text from Colossians teaches and reminds us that everything is sustained by Christ. You are sitting here in this moment because He is holding the universe together. He is, by His mercy, keeping the sun the exact distance it needs to be from the earth. He is the One keeping the blood flowing through your body. He holds all things together.

HE IS ALSO THE HEAD OF THE BODY, THE CHURCH;
He started the church. He is the One who sustains His church. He is the One who keeps us to Himself, who holds on to us despite all our sin and all the junk in our lives. He is the head of the body of Christ.

HE IS THE BEGINNING, THE FIRSTBORN FROM THE DEAD...
Just as the firstborn of creation indicates Jesus' rank as the One above all creation and the One who owns all creation—the firstborn from the dead speaks to His supremacy in the resurrection. He is the One who conquered death and has ushered in a new after-death existence for those who follow Him. There is no one greater.

SO THAT HE MIGHT COME TO HAVE FIRST PLACE IN EVERYTHING.
Jesus desires to be first in your life, to have first place over everything in your life. Just as He is the head over all creation, the head over His church, the head over all things, He insists on having first place in your life. He does not want to be a phase in your life, but rather the ruler over all of your life. He is not content to be something you are into for a season or something you think you will get to later. Christ does not want to be a part of your life, but the King over all of your life. He is not a supplement, something we just add to our already full lives. He is not a consultant to give you advice when you think you need it. He is the King who wants first place in everything. His insistence on being first place in everything is good for you.

Because you are giving up less than the best to enjoy Him—who is ultimate.

FOR GOD WAS PLEASED TO HAVE ALL HIS FULLNESS DWELL IN HIM.
Because Jesus is fully God, the holiness, righteousness, power, providence, and sovereignty of God dwell fully in Jesus. The love, mercy, compassion, grace, and kindness of God dwell fully in Jesus. And what is absolutely amazing is that when we become Christians, we dwell in Jesus, too.

What are the false perceptions of Christ in our world today? How are you living or speaking to defy those perceptions?

DAY TWO
There Is Now No Condemnation

Many refer to Romans 8 as the greatest chapter in the entire Bible. All Scripture is God breathed, so there is not one verse more holy or authoritative than another, but Romans 8 is filled with great news about what Christ has accomplished on our behalf. As the apostles wrote letters to the churches, they continually reminded the believers what Christ had accomplished in His life, death, and resurrection. Because Christ is the center of the story, the apostles preached Him over and over again. Today, let's look at Romans 8:1-4.

Therefore, there is now no condemnation for those in Christ Jesus, because the law of the Spirit of life in Christ Jesus has set you free from the law of sin and of death. For what the law could not do since it was weakened by the flesh, God did. He condemned sin in the flesh by sending his own Son in the likeness of sinful flesh as a sin offering, in order that the law's requirement would be fulfilled in us who do not walk according to the flesh but according to the Spirit.
Romans 8:1-4

No condemnation now exists for those in Christ Jesus! Condemnation is a legal term that speaks to both the declaration of guilt and the punishment associated with that guilt. So, for example, if you are caught speeding, your condemnation includes both being declared guilty of going 68 in a 55-mph zone and receiving the punishment for that offense.

While we deserve condemnation from God because we are sinners, there now exists no condemnation. Condemnation has ceased. All of God's wrath and condemnation has been replaced with His love and mercy toward you. And it is not as if His wrath is on you when you have a bad day or struggle with sin. His wrath, His condemnation, is no more. It has been replaced with His righteousness.

The opposite legal term of condemnation is justification. A judge either declares a person to be condemned or declares a person to be justified. There is no condemnation for those of us who are in Christ because Christ justified us. So why is there no condemnation?

The Story of God

Review Romans 8:1-4.

There is no condemnation for those of us in Christ because the Holy Spirit grabbed our hearts and changed us, setting us free from "the law of sin and death" (v. 2).

The phrase "the law of sin and of death" refers to the general principle that sin has corrupted all of us and that our sin leads to death. We were trapped, imprisoned by sin and death. But the Holy Spirit changed us (the Spirit's law of life).

The law God gave His people in the Old Testament was not bad, it was just powerless to change anyone. It can't save us from our sins; it can only point to our need for a Savior. That's why God sent His own Son in the flesh to be a sin offering. Just as sacrifices in the Old Testament were offered to God so He would be merciful to the people, Christ is our sin offering. Instead of condemning you, God condemned sin in the flesh of Jesus. Your sin was removed from you and placed on Jesus who took your punishment in His flesh. There is no condemnation for you because your sin was condemned in Christ.

And there is more. Because Jesus perfectly obeyed the law, His obedience is given to you in place of your sin. You have fulfilled the law's requirements because Christ's obedience is now yours.

How do we know if we are His? As verse 4 says, those who are His are those who walk with Him, who become more like Him, who walk with the Spirit and don't spend their lives living in the flesh for the things of this world.

For people like that, there is absolutely no condemnation!

How would you explain Romans 8:1-4 to someone who's never heard the gospel?

DAY THREE
Who We Are

Persecution of Christians was very intense during the early days of the Christian faith. When Rome burned to the ground, some believed the Roman emperor Nero had lit fire to his own city so he could launch new building projects. Nero needed someone to blame, and he chose the Christians. As a result, persecution escalated and Christians were dispersed throughout "Pontus, Galatia, Cappadocia, Asia, and Bithynia" (1 Pet. 1:1) and wondered how to live while surrounded by disdain in a world that is not really home. The apostle Peter reminded them who they were, of their great identity as followers of Christ. His words are true of all who belong to Christ.

As you read 1 Peter 2:9-12, circle the phrases that describe our identity, such as "chosen race."

But you are a chosen race, a royal priesthood, a holy nation, a people for his possession, so that you may proclaim the praises of the one who called you out of darkness into his marvelous light. Once you were not a people, but now you are God's people; you had not received mercy, but now you have received mercy.

Dear friends, I urge you as strangers and exiles to abstain from sinful desires that wage war against the soul. Conduct yourselves honorably among the Gentiles, so that when they slander you as evildoers, they will observe your good works and will glorify God on the day he visits.
1 Peter 2:9-12

This passage is incredibly rich.

CHOSEN RACE
Just as God chose to set His affection upon Israel in the Old Testament, God has set His love and affection upon you. You belong to Him because of His promise to you, not because of your goodness. As chosen people, we should rejoice that we belong to Him.

ROYAL PRIESTHOOD
When God instituted the tabernacle system, only the high priest was allowed to enter the Most Holy Place and be in the presence of God. But now we are royal priests. Christ's death opened a new and living way for us to enter into God's presence anytime, anywhere. As royal priests, we should enjoy His presence.
HOLY NATION

God adopted and set Israel apart as His own. As Christians, God has formed us as a new people and declared us to be holy. Because He is holy and has declared us to be holy, we are to live holy lives.

PEOPLE FOR HIS POSSESSION
We no longer belong to ourselves. We are His, which is far better than being slaves to our sin and slaves to ourselves.

STRANGERS AND EXILES
Peter reminded believers that the reason we often feel like we don't fit in this world is because we don't. This world is no longer our home, so we are to abstain from indulging in the sinfulness of this fallen world.

In these verses, Peter used the phrase "so that" twice. We have been given this great identity so that:

"So that you may proclaim the praises of the one who called you out of darkness into his marvelous light" (v. 9).

"So that when they slander you as evildoers, they will observe your good works and will glorify God on the day he visits" (v. 12).

God gave us a great identity so that we can proclaim His praises to the world. We are surrounded by people who speak against us and the Christian faith. But we are to live good lives so that those far from God may observe us and, by God's grace, be brought to faith in Christ. Then they will join us in glorifying God when He returns.

He is returning. When He does, all that is wrong will be made right. And those who know Him will spend eternity with Him. Until then, we live in a world that is not ours on a mission He has given us. Because of who we are, we are to declare His praises and live honorably among those who do not know Him.

What is the mission Christ has given us? How does our identity as explained in 1 Peter 2 affect our mission? Explain.

DAY FOUR
How We Should Live

If you are a parent, you have likely tried multiple ways to motivate your kids: threats of punishment, promises of rewards, wielding your authority, and reminding them of all you have done for them. In many ways, pastoring a group of people is a lot like parenting. When the apostles wrote letters to the churches, they cared deeply for the people receiving them and viewed themselves as their fathers in the faith.

How did the apostles strive to motivate people to live in response to God's greatness and grace? How did they encourage them to live the reality of their new identity?

The apostles often rooted the imperatives (the commands) God gave in the indicative (what Christ has done). To understand their letters, it is helpful to understand the difference between imperatives and the indicative.

Imperative = Commands or "Do"

Indicative = What Christ accomplished or "Done"

You will find that the apostles' letters are filled with imperatives, but these imperatives are grounded in what Christ has done (indicative). That's because if our hearts are not refreshed and renewed with what Christ has done for us, our hearts are unable to obey Him. We need to be in awe of His grace to be motivated to live out the commands (the imperatives).

Let's look at some passages written to the churches. Write *imperative* or *indicative* on each blank line. (The first one is completed as an example.)

Husbands, love your wives imperative ***just as Christ loved the church and gave Himself for her.*** indicative
Ephesians 5:25

What should we say then? Should we continue in sin so that grace may multiply? Absolutely not! How can we who died to sin still live in it?
Romans 6:1-2

And be kind and compassionate to one another, _____ forgiving one another, just as God also forgave you in Christ. _____
Ephesians 4:32

Therefore welcome one another, _____ just as Christ also welcomed you, _____ to the glory of God.
Romans 15:7

Now as you excel in everything—in faith, speech, knowledge, and in all diligence, and in your love for us—excel also in this act of grace [in giving]. _____ For you know the grace of our Lord Jesus Christ: Though he was rich, for your sake he became poor, so that by his poverty you might become rich. _____
2 Corinthians 8:7,9

Do you see the common theme? The imperatives are there—Do this, but they are always rooted in the indicative—because Christ has done that. As your heart is constantly refreshed with what Christ has done, you want to obey Him. You want to follow Him. His commands don't feel like a burden because this world is less and less attractive to you as you view Him as greater and greater.

Week 8: A Better Beginning

Let's close with this example: We are to think of others first (imperative) because Christ put our salvation ahead of His comfort (indicative).

Do nothing out of selfish ambition or conceit, but in humility consider others as more important than yourselves. Everyone should look not to his own interests, but rather to the interests of others.
Adopt the same attitude as that of Christ Jesus,
who, existing in the form of God,
did not consider equality with God
as something to be exploited.
Instead he emptied himself
by assuming the form of a servant,
taking on the likeness of humanity.
And when he had come as a man
he humbled himself by becoming obedient
to the point of death—
even to death on a cross.
For this reason God highly exalted him
and gave him the name
that is above every name,
so that at the name of Jesus
every knee will bow—
in heaven and on earth
and under the earth—
and every tongue will confess
that Jesus Christ is Lord,
to the glory of God the Father.
Philippians 2:3-11

What's the difference in an imperative and an indicative? Explain.

What are some examples of indicatives that motivate you? Why do they motivate you?

What happens if we get the imperative before the indicative? Explain.

REFLECT

 Before attending the group session, look back over the timeline and four days of personal study. Use this space to write down any thoughts, questions, or prayers related to redemptive history and the Bible's overarching story.

GROUP SESSION

WEEK 8

A Better Beginning

In this final group session, we'll see how the rescue of Jesus and the formation of a new people does not mean "everyone lived happily ever after... The end." The story of God continues even today! A time is coming where God's people—people from every tribe, tongue, and nation who have been rescued by Christ—will enjoy Him and His rule forever in perfect harmony. Satan will be crushed, the effects of sin will be reversed, and all things will be made new. This is where we all live today, "already, but not yet" fully experiencing a better beginning to life with God.

 Open your time together in prayer, asking God to help you understand and apply the truth revealed in His Word.

LEADERS: Sign in to the Rooted Network Digital Hub and stream this week's teaching video.

EVERYONE: Use the following pages for notes and group discussion.

Week 8 Teaching Outline

Four things we see about the better beginning:

1. The nations are gathered.

2. The curse is reversed.

3. Evil is destroyed.

4. Christ is enjoyed.

Discussion Guide

Be sure to make time for discussing everyone's insights, highlights, and changes from the entire journey through Scripture.

Don't forget to point out the discipleship experience following this last session. You'll practice sharing your stories with each other. Then, follow up with each other to celebrate experiences with sharing the story of God with other people.

1. Share a quick summary of highlights from Weeks 1-7. Why is this week an important point in redemptive history and the unfolding story of God?

2. What did Eric mean when he said that the end of the story is just a better beginning? Explain.

3. How has the curse affected you personally? Explain.

4. What did Eric mean when he said the curse will be reversed?

5. What does it mean that Jesus is the centerpiece of heaven?

6. Eric said, "Heaven isn't just for people who don't want to go to hell." What did he mean? Is he describing you? Why or why not?

Look up Philippians 2:3-11 from Day 4 (p. 136). Read it aloud.

7. How does this scripture summarize the story of God? What gospel truths are mentioned. How does it point to our better beginning?

Look back over the personal study.

8. What else was especially meaningful or helpful? How does it clarify your identity and purpose in the story of God?

Day 1: Christ Is Above All

Day 2: There Is Now No Condemnation

Day 3: Who We Are

Day 4: How We Should Live

Day 5: Reflection

9. Look back at the survey in Week 1 (p. 12). Where have you grown: in your comfort level with reading the Bible, discussing the Bible, neither, or both? Give one example of a new way you can point to what the Bible is all about: Jesus.

10. How does the takeaway affect your view of Scripture? How will you respond to this part of the story?

11. In what other ways have you grown in your understanding and application of the gospel through this Deep Dive study? Be specific.

Takeaway:
We can live in the "messy middle" because we know the glorious ending.

Week 8: A Better Beginning

EXPERIENCE 2: JOIN THE STORY

 See Appendix B: Experiential Discipleship to prepare for this time of sharing your story.

Following Jesus is more than just knowing facts about the Bible—it's an experience. You get to join this epic adventure. God is inviting and empowering you to live it and share it with confidence. Everyone needs to hear the good news of the gospel. Jesus changes lives. He's working in your life and in other people's lives too.

This week, look for an opportunity to share your story with someone you interact with or see on a regular basis. It may come up in a casual conversation; it doesn't need to be forced. After you have shared, reflect on how God showed up as you shared. How did it go? What did you learn? No matter how you think it went, thank God for giving you an opportunity to share your story as part of His story. Pray He will continue to move in the life of the person you shared with, and pray He will open up more opportunities for conversation.

Here are some other helpful tips about sharing your story with others:

Be Relational
Don't think of sharing your story as a goal to accomplish—think of the person. Jesus' love flowing through you to other people is the priority. Relationship is key.

Write It Out
Think of your story like a drama (or maybe a comedy) with three parts. Using the next page, write your story in bullet points that you can use as the main ideas when you share. Then, practice sharing your story using a timer. Try to keep it under three minutes. This leaves room for you to listen to others and answer any questions they may have. Don't eliminate the passion or emotion from your story. Remember to acknowledge God's faithfulness and your need for Christ, His forgiveness, and His grace. Now you have a summary of your faith journey that is easy to remember, easy to share, and an easy way to invite others to join the story of God through faith.

Translate It for Your Audience
Try to take out any "Christian-ese" or "church words" and phrases that can alienate the person you are talking to, or at the very least, confuse them and keep them from identifying with your story (words like "gospel" and "repent"). Replace them with words that are more relatable and conversational ("good news" and "turn to God").

Prayerfully lean into points you think will resonate with the person you are sharing with. Ask God: "What part of my story will connect with their story?"

Who might need to hear the the story of God—the gospel revealed in Scripture?

What points in your story might be most meaningful to them?

Part 1: My life before . . .
Think through areas of conflict in your story (a lie, sin, struggle, etc.) in which you have experienced growth. It could be something you believed, something you felt, or a way you chose to live. Refer back to the *Break the Cycle* experience on p. 72-73 for ideas.

Part 2: How God's story changed my story . . .
What happened that began the transformation from Part 1 to Part 3? Was it an experience in your church, your small group, or in this study? Maybe someone showed you the love of Jesus at just the right time in your life. How does it relate to better understanding the story of God? Find a natural way to point to Scripture.

Part 3: My life now . . .
Think of how God has grown you in that particular area (especially over the last eight weeks) and about what is different because of His work in you. What do you now believe and know is true? How do you feel today? How do you live your life differently? How does the biblical story give you a new identity and hope for the future? Remember, the best is yet to come!

Deep(er) Dive

Appendix A: The 7 Rhythms of a Disciple — 148

Appendix B: Experiential Discipleship — 150
Experience 1: Break the Cycle
Experience 2: Join the Story

Appendix C: FAQs — 153
When Thinking about Scripture

Appendix D: Words Theologians Use — 154
When Talking about Scripture

Appendix E: Chronological Bible Reading Plan — 156
365-Day Checklist

Additional Reading — 162

Appendix A: The 7 Rhythms of a Disciple

Grounded in God's Word, the *7 Rhythms* are foundational to Rooted Network discipleship resources like this one. Each of these rhythms was practiced by the early church in Acts 2. When we commit to practicing the *7 Rhythms* in community like the early church, we see growth and transformation in both our personal lives and in our communities.

Daily Devotion (Acts 2:42, 46)
Scripture is the very Word of God. Through it, He equips us with all we need to learn about Him and live a life pleasing to Him. A daily rhythm of reading, meditating on, and applying God's Word to our lives is key.

Prayer (Acts 2:42)
One of the most important elements in any healthy relationship is communication. Prayer is just that: engaging God in a conversation, sharing our hearts with Him, and spending time listening to His voice, both individually and in community.

Repentance (Acts 2:37-39)
Jesus saves those who believe and call upon His name. Saving grace is once and for all (justification) and also a continual invitation to repent for our wrongdoings. With the help of the Spirit we take inventory of our lives, humbly and honestly confess our sin, and turn away from our sin toward God in surrender. Through Jesus' offer of forgiveness, we receive true freedom.

Sacrificial Generosity (Acts 2:44-45)
Giving demonstrates our dependence on God. We acknowledge that all we own has been given to us by Him. In His generosity toward us, God desires that we, too, are generous and will use our resources as a tangible way to partner with Him in His work in the world and in the lives of those around us. We are blessed to be a blessing (Gen. 12:2).

Serve the Community (Acts 2:44-45)
We are called and equipped by the Holy Spirit to share God's love by participating in the ministry of Jesus. He has given us agency with Him to fearlessly influence our society and the world. When we serve in the world and in His Church, we impact those around us and reveal God's glory.

Share Your Story (Acts 2:14-36)
The greatest gift we can ever give someone who doesn't yet know Jesus is an introduction to Him. Sharing our life stories is the most powerful way to show the transforming power and salvation offered through Jesus Christ. When we tell our stories of transformation, we tell the story of God.

Worship (Acts 2:26-28, 46-47)
As children of God, it is important to consistently set aside time to remember what God has done, to thank Him for it, and to put Him on display as we give Him the glory. In all circumstances, we are called to practice God-centered worship.

---

*For more about the *7 Rhythms*, including samples of **Rooted**, a 10-week group-discipleship experience designed for churches, visit **experiencerooted.com**.

Appendix B: Experiential Discipleship

Discipleship is experiential learning—knowing and doing what Jesus taught and modeled. We are called to follow Christ. The Christian life is one of faith in action.

Too often, Christian discipleship or "disciple making" focuses on *knowing*, with less emphasis on *doing*. According to this approach, what Christians should do will naturally flow out of what they know. In other words, teach people the right things and they'll begin doing the right things too. This is a particularly "Western" approach to knowledge and learning. Certainly, there is some truth to this; however, historically and even presently in many cultures, doing something is the primary method of teaching and learning. In this approach, a person truly knows something only after they've experienced it.

Discipleship is not passively learning information about the Christian life—it's not just studying the Bible.

Discipleship is participating in the life-transformation throughout the Christian life—it's joining others in the story of God.

This Deep Dive study includes two intentional experiences outside of the regular group time. The following tips will help you make the most out of the experience.

Brainstorm possible times and places for your experience following Week 4. (Read the tips on the next page for Experience 1: Break the Cycle.)

Brainstorm possible times and places for your experience following Week 8. (Read the tips on the following page for Experience 2: Join the Story.)

Experience 1: Break the Cycle (Following Week 4)

At the halfway point in your journey through the story of God, set aside time for intentional repentance and breaking of strongholds or patterns of sin revealing a lack of trust in God's goodness. This experience sets up the transition between the Old and New Testament—positioned between the period of judges and kings and the final season of exile and return before the coming of Jesus.

Remember: Plan ahead to make the most of this experience. Encourage everyone to participate.

- Do not skip or shorten the time of teaching and discussion for Week 8. Schedule additional time for group members to meet. You have two good options:

  1. The best time for people may be after the regular group session, extending your time by at least 30 minutes, ideally an hour.

  2. You may be able to schedule a separate time to connect for this experience—in that case smaller groups of people can meet at their convenience.

- Organize everyone into smaller groups of 2-3 people. Ideally, group members can choose their own partners for the experience. Depending on group dynamics, you can assign or suggest pairings. The important thing is for people to feel a level of confidentiality and a lack of judgment. Be sure to emphasize those things.

- Be sure that everyone has their own space to focus on the experience without distraction. Instruct everyone to read and prayerfully reflect on pages 72-73. Emphasize the importance of being quiet before the LORD, listening to whatever the Spirit reveals to each person. Remind group members of God's love for them individually and as a family, brothers and sisters in Christ.

- Emphasize the power of the final step—expressing specific areas of repentance with a trusted brothers or sisters in Christ and, if needed, humbly confessing specific sin against another person and asking for their forgiveness.

- To ensure sufficient space for personal reflection and sharing with each other, determine approximate times for both parts of this experience. Feel free to set a timer on your phone or watch, but try not to look at, touch, or listen to any devices. Silencing any alerts or setting your phone to airplane mode can help you focus on your experience with God and each other.

Experience 2: Join the Story (Following Week 8)

Following the completion of this epic journey through Scripture, group members should have a clear picture of the overarching story of God. This chronological overview of redemptive history equips us for a more holistic and comprehensive grasp of the gospel—the whole Bible points us to Jesus. This experience leads participants in a simple exercise for developing their personal testimonies with tips on how to share their stories with others. As followers of Jesus their own stories are part of His bigger story and the best is yet to come! We should be eager to invite others to join us in relationship with God and His family of faith.

- Do not skip or shorten the time of teaching and discussion for Week 8. Schedule additional time for group members to meet. You have two options:

    1. Schedule an additional week at the usual meeting time. This option allows people opportunities to share their stories with someone in their daily lives before celebrating those conversations as a group.

    2. Extend your group time for Week 8. This option allows everyone time to develop their stories and to practice sharing them with each other, growing more comfortable with conversational evangelism and disciple making.

- This is a great opportunity for the smaller groups of 2–3 from the first experience to get back together as a natural way to celebrate growth and progress. Point out the natural relationship between the rhythms of repentance and sharing your story—they both deepen our love for God and people through steps of faith.

- If possible, set aside time for each group member to share their 3-part story, with the whole group and celebrate God's work in their lives.

- Ask the Spirit to put someone on your heart and look for opportunities to reach out to someone new, reconnect with someone, or deepen a relationship with a casual acquaintance.

- Pray for the ability to discern any natural opportunities to share the gospel or talk about things that God has been teaching you. Be patient; don't force any topic or conversation.

- When sharing your story, engage the other person in conversation by asking questions about their interests and activities. Don't be shy about asking for a response to what you shared: What resonates with them? Would they want to join the story of God by experiencing the freedom of a new identity and purpose found only in Jesus?

- Do more than simply check this off the to-do list. Make plans to reconnect. Remember that this the greatest mission and purpose in life—inviting people to join the story of God as part of His family through faith in Jesus.

Appendix C: FAQs

How did we get the Bible?
God inspired and sustained the Scripture for His glory and our good. The 66 books in the Bible are known by theologians as "the canon of Scripture." As Christ-followers, it is our "rule of faith," our authority for what we believe and how we live. The Scripture contains thirty-nine books in the Old Testament and twenty-seven books in the New Testament. When Jesus walked this earth, there was deep agreement among the Jewish people that the thirty-nine books in the Old Testament were God's Word. The Scriptures were preserved in the tabernacle and temple, so it was obvious and transparent to all that those books were embraced as God's Word. Jesus and the New Testament biblical writers quoted the Old Testament often.

When it comes to the twenty-seven books in the New Testament, we have the gospels, the accounts of Jesus, letters that apostles wrote to churches, and the book of Revelation. For a book to "pass the inspiration test" and be included in "the canon," the writer had to be an apostle (one who saw Jesus), the teaching in the book had to be acknowledged by the early church as authentic and inspired, and the doctrine of the book had to be in alignment with the whole of Scripture. In the Old Testament, God used the temple to hold the canon together. With the New Testament, God has used His living temple—the Church.

What about all the different versions of the Bible?
The Old Testament was written in Hebrew. The New Testament was written in Koine Greek. The Bible has thankfully been translated into our language. The versions of the Bible are very similar to one another and differ on how the scholars who worked on that version translate a word from the original language into English. For example, the word *hesed* in Hebrew may be translated as "faithful love" by one version and "loving kindness" by another translation.

Which version of the Bible is the best?
Whichever one you will read! Seriously! Some versions translate word for word from the original language. Some versions translate phrase for phrase. And some versions are updated translations from a previous version.

Isn't using the Bible to vouch for the Bible circular reasoning?
Christians often use the Scripture to point to the inspiration of the Scripture. It is because, for Christians, there is not a higher authority to appeal to. At the same time, there are numerous prophecies that were written in the Old Testament that were fulfilled in history—such as Israel being divided into two kingdoms and the King of Persia being identified years before his reign began. And there are numerous prophecies about Jesus that were historically fulfilled—such as His birth in Bethlehem and His death by crucifixion. Additionally, there are far more and better-preserved manuscripts of the biblical text than other historical and religious documents.

Appendix D: Words Theologians Use

WHEN TALKING ABOUT SCRIPTURE

Verbal Plenary Inspiration

The Bible contains 66 books from 40 different human authors, but according to this verse there is really only one ultimate Author – God Himself. Yes, God used humans to write the words down and used their personalities, their backgrounds, and their gifting just as He uses people today. But God's Spirit was the one carrying the prophets along as they spoke and wrote (2 Pet. 1:20-21). There is a theological term that is often used to describe the words in Scripture. Brace yourself. It is a bit nerdy: Verbal Plenary Inspiration. The term may need some unpacking:

- **Verbal:** The words of God were given and recorded in the Scripture. Not just ideas but every single word in the Scripture was given by God for His people. Jesus, in His teaching, quoted from 24 different books in the Old Testament. And Jesus spoke with confidence about even every letter in the Old Testament. He told a crowd of people: "Don't think that I came to abolish the Law or the Prophets. I did not come to abolish but to fulfill. For truly I tell you, until heaven and earth pass away, not the smallest letter or one stroke of a letter will pass away from the law until all things are accomplished." (Matt. 5:17-18)

- **Plenary:** The entire Bible is the Word of God. The Bible does not become the Word of God for us based on how we feel about it. The Bible does not contain the words of God and other words too. No, the Bible is the inspired and, therefore, authoritative Word of God.

- **Inspiration:** The words of God in the entirety of the Bible are God-breathed.

Why it matters: *You can read your Bible with confidence that each word was given by God to you. Yes, those words have been translated from the original language but God has preserved His Word for your benefit. You are not reading something that is merely good advice or wisdom from this age. You are reading the Word of God.*

Authority

The words in Scripture are God's words and His words have authority over our lives just as God has authority over our lives. God's words are true and faithful because God is true and faithful (2 Pet. 1:21; John 17:17).

Why it matters: *Your life is best-lived when you place yourself under the authority of Scripture.*

Necessity

The Scripture is necessary for knowing God personally through Jesus Christ and for growing in one's relationship with God (Rom. 10:13-17; James 1:18; Col. 3:16-17).

Why it matters: *You need the Scripture to know the gospel and to grow as a Christ-follower.*

Clarity

The Scripture is for everyone and can be understood by anyone who is humble enough to seek help from God's Word (Ps. 19:7; Matt. 4:4).

Why it matters: *While some passages are difficult to understand, you can read and understand the Bible.*

Sufficiency

God's Word does not fail in the lives of those who seek Him, and the Scripture prepares you for every good work in this life (Isa. 55:10-11; 2 Tim. 3:16-17).

Why it matters: *The Scripture contains everything you need to learn to trust and obey God.*

---

*For a deep dive into the theological foundation of our Christian faith and practical ways those core doctrines shape our daily lives, download a sample of **Theology and the Mission of God** by Eric Geiger and Ed Stetzer at **experiencerooted.com/deepdive**.

Appendix E: Chronological Bible Reading Plan

Now that you've completed this Deep Dive study, you hopefully have a better understanding of the overarching storyline of Scripture. *The Story of God* was created to help you see Christ throughout biblical history. Obviously, we couldn't cover all 66 books of the Bible in an 8-week study, so here's a great next step as you continue the epic journey through Scripture: Read it all.

The following is a 1-year / 365-day reading plan to walk you through the entire Bible in chronological order. You may want to invite a friend, family member, or person from your small group to join you for accountability and conversation—every adventure is better with a traveling companion! There's no pressure to complete it in exactly 1 year. Journey at your own pace.

Keep in mind that the books (and even some sections within the books) of the Bible represent a variety of genres, topics, time periods, and authors. You'll notice some slight differences between popular reading plans, but the few distinctions are generally minor preferenes not affecting the storyline of Scripture. The approach taken for organizing this particular reading plan is keeping it simple—rarely reading from more than one book in a day, never splitting up chapters into selected verses, and always limited to a few chapters at a time based on length. This will help you keep your attention on stories with natural breaks in your reading at the end of a chapter.

Finally, there's a good chance you have the YouVersion Bible app on your phone already since it's by far the most popular Bible app. It's full of helpful and convenient features, including a huge selection of reading plans. Those are also a great option for reading through the Bible chronologically (and in other ways) individually or with other people. However you choose to read through the Bible, I strongly encourage you to make it a goal worth accomplishing. If you've never read the entire Bible, you'll be surprised at how much you start looking forward to it, even if it feels like a daunting task now. There's a good chance that it becomes a regular part of your Christian life for years to come.

Daily Devotion, one of the 7 Rhythms of a Disciple, is a proven way to dive deeper into your faith. So, let's get started!

	#	Reading		#	Reading
☐	1	Genesis 1-3	☐	37	Exodus 22-24
☐	2	Genesis 4-6	☐	38	Exodus 25-27
☐	3	Genesis 7-11	☐	39	Exodus 28-29
☐	4	Job 1-5	☐	40	Exodus 30-32
☐	5	Job 6-8	☐	41	Exodus 33-35
☐	6	Job 9-11	☐	42	Exodus 36-38
☐	7	Job 12-14	☐	43	Exodus 39-40
☐	8	Job 15-19	☐	44	Leviticus 1-3
☐	9	Job 20-24	☐	45	Leviticus 4-7
☐	10	Job 25-27	☐	46	Leviticus 8-10
☐	11	Job 28-31	☐	47	Leviticus 11-13
☐	12	Job 32-34	☐	48	Leviticus 14-15
☐	13	Job 35-37	☐	49	Leviticus 16-18
☐	14	Job 38-39	☐	50	Leviticus 19-21
☐	15	Job 40-42	☐	51	Leviticus 22-23
☐	16	Genesis 12-15	☐	52	Leviticus 24-25
☐	17	Genesis 16-18	☐	53	Leviticus 26-27
☐	18	Genesis 19-21	☐	54	Numbers 1-2
☐	19	Genesis 22-24	☐	55	Numbers 3-4
☐	20	Genesis 25-26	☐	56	Numbers 5-6
☐	21	Genesis 27-29	☐	57	Numbers 7
☐	22	Genesis 30-31	☐	58	Numbers 8-10
☐	23	Genesis 32-34	☐	59	Numbers 11-13
☐	24	Genesis 35-37	☐	60	Numbers 14-15; Psalm 90
☐	25	Genesis 38-40	☐	61	Numbers 16-17
☐	26	Genesis 41-42	☐	62	Numbers 18-20
☐	27	Genesis 43-45	☐	63	Numbers 21-22
☐	28	Genesis 46-47	☐	64	Numbers 23-25
☐	29	Genesis 48-50	☐	65	Numbers 26-27
☐	30	Exodus 1-3	☐	66	Numbers 28-30
☐	31	Exodus 4-6	☐	67	Numbers 31-32
☐	32	Exodus 7-9	☐	68	Numbers 33-34
☐	33	Exodus 10-12	☐	69	Numbers 35-36
☐	34	Exodus 13-15	☐	70	Deuteronomy 1-2
☐	35	Exodus 16-18	☐	71	Deuteronomy 3-4
☐	36	Exodus 19-21	☐	72	Deuteronomy 5-7

Appendix E: Chronological Bible Reading Plan

☐	73	Deuteronomy 8-10	☐	110	Psalms 121, 123-125, 128-130
☐	74	Deuteronomy 11-13	☐	111	2 Samuel 1-4
☐	75	Deuteronomy 14-16	☐	112	Psalms 6, 8-10, 14, 16, 19, 21
☐	76	Deuteronomy 17-20	☐	113	1 Chronicles 1-2
☐	77	Deuteronomy 21-23	☐	114	Psalms 43-45, 49, 84-85, 87
☐	78	Deuteronomy 24-27	☐	115	1 Chronicles 3-5
☐	79	Deuteronomy 28-29	☐	116	Psalms 73, 77-78
☐	80	Deuteronomy 30-31	☐	117	1 Chronicles 6
☐	81	Deuteronomy 32-34; Psalm 91	☐	118	Psalms 81, 88, 92-93
☐	82	Joshua 1-3	☐	119	1 Chronicles 7-10
☐	83	Joshua 4-8	☐	120	Psalms 102-104
☐	84	Joshua 9-11	☐	121	2 Samuel 5; 1 Chronicles 11-12
☐	85	Joshua 12-15	☐	122	Psalm 133
☐	86	Joshua 16-18	☐	123	Psalms 106-107
☐	87	Joshua 19-21	☐	124	1 Chronicles 13-16
☐	88	Joshua 22-24	☐	125	Psalms 1-2, 15, 22-24, 47, 68
☐	89	Judges 1-2	☐	126	Psalms 89, 96, 100-101, 105, 132
☐	90	Judges 3-5	☐	127	2 Samuel 6-7; 1 Chronicles 17
☐	91	Judges 6-7	☐	128	Psalms 25, 29, 33, 36, 39
☐	92	Judges 8-9	☐	129	2 Samuel 8-9; 1 Chronicles 18
☐	93	Judges 10-12	☐	130	Psalms 50, 53, 60, 75
☐	94	Judges 13-15	☐	131	2 Samuel 10; 1 Chronicles 19; Psalm 20
☐	95	Judges 16-18	☐	132	Psalms 65-67, 69-70
☐	96	Judges 19-21	☐	133	2 Samuel 11-12; 1 Chronicles 20
☐	97	Ruth	☐	134	Psalms 32, 51, 86, 122
☐	98	1 Samuel 1-3	☐	135	2 Samuel 13-15
☐	99	1 Samuel 4-8	☐	136	Psalms 3-4, 12-13, 28, 55
☐	100	1 Samuel 9-12	☐	137	2 Samuel 16-18
☐	101	1 Samuel 13-14	☐	138	Psalms 26, 40, 58, 61-62, 64
☐	102	1 Samuel 15-17	☐	139	2 Samuel 19-21
☐	103	1 Samuel 18-20; Psalms 11, 59	☐	140	Psalms 5, 38, 41-42
☐	104	1 Samuel 21-24	☐	141	2 Samuel 22-23; Psalm 57
☐	105	Psalms 7, 27, 31, 34, 52	☐	142	Psalms 95, 97-99
☐	106	Psalms 56, 120, 140-142	☐	143	2 Samuel 24; 1 Chronicles 21-22; Psalm 30
☐	107	1 Samuel 25-27	☐	144	Psalms 108-110
☐	108	Psalms 17, 35, 54, 63	☐	145	1 Chronicles 23-25
☐	109	1 Samuel 28-31; Psalm 18	☐	146	Psalms 131, 138-139, 143-145

	#	Reading
☐	147	1 Chronicles 26-29; Psalm 127
☐	148	Psalms 111-118
☐	149	1 Kings 1-2; Psalms 37, 71, 94
☐	150	Psalm 119
☐	151	1 Kings 3-4
☐	152	2 Chronicles 1; Psalm 72
☐	153	Song of Solomon
☐	154	Proverbs 1-3
☐	155	Proverbs 4-6
☐	156	Proverbs 7-9
☐	157	Proverbs 10-12
☐	158	Proverbs 13-15
☐	159	Proverbs 16-18
☐	160	Proverbs 19-21
☐	161	Proverbs 22-24
☐	162	1 Kings 5-6; 2 Chronicles 2-3
☐	163	1 Kings 7; 2 Chronicles 4
☐	164	1 Kings 8; 2 Chronicles 5
☐	165	2 Chronicles 6-7; Psalm 136
☐	166	Psalms 134, 146-150
☐	167	1 Kings 9; 2 Chronicles 8
☐	168	Proverbs 25-26
☐	169	Proverbs 27-29
☐	170	Ecclesiastes 1-6
☐	171	Ecclesiastes 7-12
☐	172	1 Kings 10-11; 2 Chronicles 9
☐	173	Proverbs 30-31
☐	174	1 Kings 12-14
☐	175	2 Chronicles 10-12
☐	176	1 Kings 15; 2 Chronicles 13-16
☐	177	1 Kings 16; 2 Chronicles 17
☐	178	1 Kings 17-19
☐	179	1 Kings 20-21
☐	180	1 Kings 22; 2 Chronicles 18
☐	181	2 Chronicles 19-23
☐	182	Obadiah; Psalms 82-83
☐	183	2 Kings 1-4
☐	184	2 Kings 5-8
☐	185	2 Kings 9-11
☐	186	2 Kings 12-13; 2 Chronicles 24
☐	187	2 Kings 14; 2 Chronicles 25
☐	188	Jonah
☐	189	2 Kings 15; 2 Chronicles 26
☐	190	Isaiah 1-4
☐	191	Isaiah 5-8
☐	192	Amos 1-5
☐	193	Amos 6-9
☐	194	2 Chronicles 27; Isaiah 9-12
☐	195	Micah
☐	196	2 Chronicles 28; 2 Kings 16-17
☐	197	Isaiah 13-17
☐	198	Isaiah 18-22
☐	199	Isaiah 23-27
☐	200	2 Kings 18; 2 Chronicles 29-31; Psalm 48
☐	201	Hosea 1-7
☐	202	Hosea 8-14
☐	203	Isaiah 28-30
☐	204	Isaiah 31-34
☐	205	Isaiah 35-36
☐	206	Isaiah 37-39; Psalm 76
☐	207	Isaiah 40-43
☐	208	Isaiah 44-48
☐	209	2 Kings 19; Psalms 46, 80, 135
☐	210	Isaiah 49-53
☐	211	Isaiah 54-58
☐	212	Isaiah 59-63
☐	213	Isaiah 64-66
☐	214	2 Kings 20-21
☐	215	2 Chronicles 32-33
☐	216	Nahum
☐	217	2 Kings 22-23; 2 Chronicles 34-35
☐	218	Zephaniah
☐	219	Jeremiah 1-3
☐	220	Jeremiah 4-6

Appendix E: Chronological Bible Reading Plan

☐	221	Jeremiah 7-9	☐	258 Daniel 7-9
☐	222	Jeremiah 10-13	☐	259 Daniel 10-12
☐	223	Jeremiah 14-17	☐	260 Ezra 1-3
☐	224	Jeremiah 18-22	☐	261 Ezra 4-6; Psalm 137
☐	225	Jeremiah 23-25	☐	262 Haggai
☐	226	Jeremiah 26-29	☐	263 Zechariah 1-4
☐	227	Jeremiah 30-31	☐	264 Zechariah 5-9
☐	228	Jeremiah 32-34	☐	265 Zechariah 10-14
☐	229	Jeremiah 35-37	☐	266 Esther 1-5
☐	230	Jeremiah 38-40; Psalms 74, 79	☐	267 Esther 6-10
☐	231	2 Kings 24-25; 2 Chronicles 36	☐	268 Ezra 7-10
☐	232	Habakkuk	☐	269 Nehemiah 1-5
☐	233	Jeremiah 41-45	☐	270 Nehemiah 6-7
☐	234	Jeremiah 46-48	☐	271 Nehemiah 8-10
☐	235	Jeremiah 49-50	☐	272 Nehemiah 11-13; Psalm 126
☐	236	Jeremiah 51-52	☐	273 Malachi
☐	237	Lamentations 1-2	☐	274 Luke 1; John 1
☐	238	Lamentations 3-5	☐	275 Matthew 1; Luke 2
☐	239	Ezekiel 1-4	☐	276 Matthew 2
☐	240	Ezekiel 5-8	☐	277 Matthew 3; Mark 1; Luke 3
☐	241	Ezekiel 9-12	☐	278 Matthew 4; Luke 4-5
☐	242	Ezekiel 13-15	☐	279 John 2-4
☐	243	Ezekiel 16-17	☐	280 Matthew 8; Mark 2
☐	244	Ezekiel 18-20	☐	281 John 5
☐	245	Ezekiel 21-22	☐	282 Matthew 12; Mark 3; Luke 6
☐	246	Ezekiel 23-24	☐	283 Matthew 5-7
☐	247	Ezekiel 25-27	☐	284 Matthew 9; Luke 7
☐	248	Ezekiel 28-30	☐	285 Matthew 11
☐	249	Ezekiel 31-33	☐	286 Luke 11
☐	250	Ezekiel 34-36	☐	287 Matthew 13; Luke 8
☐	251	Ezekiel 37-39	☐	288 Mark 4-5
☐	252	Ezekiel 40-42	☐	289 Matthew 10
☐	253	Ezekiel 43-45	☐	290 Matthew 14; Mark 6; Luke 9
☐	254	Ezekiel 46-48	☐	291 John 6
☐	255	Joel	☐	292 Matthew 15; Mark 7
☐	256	Daniel 1-3	☐	293 Matthew 16; Mark 8
☐	257	Daniel 4-6	☐	294 Matthew 17; Mark 9

- [ ] **295** Matthew 18
- [ ] **296** John 7-8
- [ ] **297** John 9-10
- [ ] **298** Luke 10
- [ ] **299** Luke 12-13
- [ ] **300** Luke 14-15
- [ ] **301** Luke 16-17
- [ ] **302** John 11
- [ ] **303** Luke 18
- [ ] **304** Matthew 19; Mark 10
- [ ] **305** Matthew 20-21
- [ ] **306** Luke 19
- [ ] **307** Mark 11; John 12
- [ ] **308** Matthew 22; Mark 12
- [ ] **309** Matthew 23; Luke 20-21
- [ ] **310** Mark 13
- [ ] **311** Matthew 24
- [ ] **312** Matthew 25
- [ ] **313** Matthew 26; Mark 14
- [ ] **314** Luke 22; John 13
- [ ] **315** John 14-17
- [ ] **316** Matthew 27; Mark 15
- [ ] **317** Luke 23; John 18-19
- [ ] **318** Matthew 28; Mark 16
- [ ] **319** Luke 24; John 20-21
- [ ] **320** Acts 1-3
- [ ] **321** Acts 4-6
- [ ] **322** Acts 7-8
- [ ] **323** Acts 9-10
- [ ] **324** Acts 11-12
- [ ] **325** Acts 13-14
- [ ] **326** James
- [ ] **327** Acts 15-16
- [ ] **328** Galatians 1-3
- [ ] **329** Galatians 4-6
- [ ] **330** Acts 17
- [ ] **331** 1 & 2 Thessalonians
- [ ] **332** Acts 18-19
- [ ] **333** 1 Corinthians 1-4
- [ ] **334** 1 Corinthians 5-8
- [ ] **335** 1 Corinthians 9-11
- [ ] **336** 1 Corinthians 12-14
- [ ] **337** 1 Corinthians 15-16
- [ ] **338** 2 Corinthians 1-4
- [ ] **339** 2 Corinthians 5-9
- [ ] **340** 2 Corinthians 10-13
- [ ] **341** Romans 1-3
- [ ] **342** Romans 4-7
- [ ] **343** Romans 8-10
- [ ] **344** Romans 11-13
- [ ] **345** Romans 14-16
- [ ] **346** Acts 20-23
- [ ] **347** Acts 24-26
- [ ] **348** Acts 27-28
- [ ] **349** Colossians, Philemon
- [ ] **350** Ephesians
- [ ] **351** Philippians
- [ ] **352** 1 Timothy
- [ ] **353** Titus
- [ ] **354** 1 Peter
- [ ] **355** Hebrews 1-6
- [ ] **356** Hebrews 7-10
- [ ] **357** Hebrews 11-13
- [ ] **358** 2 Timothy
- [ ] **359** 2 Peter, Jude
- [ ] **360** 1 John
- [ ] **361** 2, 3 John
- [ ] **362** Revelation 1-5
- [ ] **363** Revelation 6-11
- [ ] **364** Revelation 12-18
- [ ] **365** Revelation 19-22

Appendix E: Chronological Bible Reading Plan

Additional Reading

The following books were extremely valuable and helpful during preparation for this Bible study. I read through them multiple times, and the authors helped form my thoughts and presentation probably more than I realize.

- *The Drama of Scripture* by Craig Bartholomew and Michael Goheen
- *God's Big Picture* by Vaughn Roberts
- *Telling God's Story* by Preben Vang and Terry Carter
- *According to Plan* by Graeme Goldsworthy
- *The God Who Is There* by D. A. Carson
- *Living God's Word* by J. Scott Duvall & J. Daniel Hays
- *From Creation to New Creation* by Tim Chester
- *A Walk Through the Bible* by Lesslie Newbigin
- *The Scarlet Thread Through the Scriptures* by W.A. Criswell
- *Seamless* by Angie Smith
- *The Cross of Christ* by John Stott

Additionally, the timeline I use throughout the study and the map of the Northern and Southern kingdom in Season 5 are adapted from the Biblical Illustrator team at LifeWay Christian Resources. The chart labeled "Cycle of Sin" in Season 4 is adapted from the chart provided by J. Scott Duvall and J. Daniel Hays in Living God's Word.

For more about the 7 Rhythms on page 127 and discipleship experiences for students and adults, preview Rooted and Rooted Essentials at experiencerooted.com.

DIVIDED KINGDOM

ISRAEL'S CAPTIVITY

ASSYRIANS 722 B.C.

BABYLONIANS 587/586 B.C.

Additional Reading

Teaching videos for *The Story of God* are included with this workbook.

To access the teaching videos, follow these steps:

1 Go to **experiencerooted.com** to log in or create an account

2 Access the Rooted Network Digital Hub by scanning the QR code or by visiting *experiencerooted.com/storyofgodvideos*

3 Before checking out, enter and apply this discount code: **SOG2WKBK7YUF3**

4 Click **REGISTER** and then **GET STARTED**

Each week, return to the Rooted Network Digital Hub at **experiencerooted.com** to access and stream *The Story of God Teaching Videos*.